ROUTLEDGE STUDIES IN ENTREPRENEURSHIP

Edited by
STUART BRUCHEY
Allan Nevins Professor Emeritus
Coumbia University

A ROUTLEDGE SERIES

MANAGING OUR MARGINS

Women Entrepreneurs In Suburbia

KIMBERLY A. REED

Routledge
Taylor & Francis Group

LONDON AND NEW YORK

First published 2001 by Routledge
2 Park Square, Milton Park, Abingdon, Oxfordshire OX14 4RN
711 Third Avenue, New York, NY, 10017

First issued in paperback 2014

Routledge is an imprint of the Taylor & Francis Group, an informa business

Copyright © 2001 by Kimberly A. Reed

Library of Congress Cataloging-in-Publication Data is available from the Library of Congress.

ISBN 13: 978-1-138-86388-0 (pbk)
ISBN 13: 978-0-8153-3992-2 (hbk)

CONTENTS

LIST OF TABLES

Preface

One morning in 1991, I found an advertising section devoted to business-es owned by women in a local newspaper in central New Jersey. To a soci-ologist this "new woman entrepreneur" was an intriguing figure. Women in the suburbs are usually portrayed as consumers, purchasing for the fam-ily, or as working commuters who struggle to balance household and work-place obligations. An independent woman producing goods and services outside of employment and outside of a family firm headed by a man chal-lenged suburban norms. I decided to interview local women who had become independent business owners. By looking behind the images and statistics, I sought to explore how business women understand their iden-tities, experiences, and the challenges they face.

When I began looking at entrepreneurship a decade ago, the new oppor-tunities created by high technology machines and systems were just begin-ning to democratize trade and commerce. Today, new opportunities for doing business in the service areas of the economy, combined with new tech-nologies such as computers, fax, net systems and mobile telecommunica-tions make it easier for millions of men and women to invest small capital resources in the organization of entrepreneurial enterprises. Yet, individuals who trade successfully must posses knowledge about products and services. Business owners must also know about local practices or the norms of trade and negotiation. This cultural knowledge is essential to establishing values and prices, but it is only gained through participation in organized groups, either industry groups, real or virtual trading communities, or voluntary associations. Women must find their way inside markets and industries where cultures are still dominated by men and larger corporate firms.

I argue that women who are entrepreneurs rely upon better employ-ment experiences and access to social resources as well as modest capital in the process of establishing their own firms. This approach stands in con-tradiction to works in social science about self-employed women, which develop from the theoretical assumption that displacement from employ-ment, or stress caused by trying to combine full time employment and other role obligations, encourage women to start their own firms. While such stresses are common, the millions of women who formed small organiza-tions over the last three decades made voluntary choices based on their per-ceptions that they could succeed in business. The search for a secure posi-tion in the economy is a challenge that confronts everyone in the middle class. Women are concerned about managing their personal lives and fam-ily obligations, but such domestic adjustments do not explain women's entrepreneurship. Women start their own firms because they finally have what it takes to operate independently, including full time work or man-agement experience and social acceptance for their public roles.

The love and shelter of my parents, Dr. James Wesley Reed and Diane Spitzfaden Reed, sustained me while I was in the field. Melanie Franklin's comments as a reader helped me to clarify my arguments. At the City University of New York Graduate Center in Manhattan, Professor Cynthia Fuchs Epstein guided this research project when it was a dissertation. The New Jersey Association of Women Business Owners allowed me to observe their meetings and to involve their members in the research process. Members of the Women's Economic Development Corporation shared their entrepreneurial histories with me. I thank these associations for helping this project, and for supporting hundreds of other people who believe that women can achieve success in business. Finally, I would like to express my gratitude to all of the participants. Throughout this book I have quoted from their interviews and conversations. Although they must remain anony-mous, these women's voices remain a lasting part of my life experience.

The Emergence of the Woman Entrepreneur in Suburbia

Women constitute a large proportion of small entrepreneurs, more than nine and a half million businesses in the United States. By 1992 they owned approximately thirty-five percent of all sole proprietorships, an increase from an estimate of less than five percent in 1972.[1] Women-owned small businesses employ twenty-four percent of the private labor force, compared to fifty-three percent of the private labor force employed by all small businesses.[2] How do women establish themselves as business owners in a country where entrepreneurship is traditionally associated with male leadership? How have women adapted to new roles as small firms owners?

In sociological studies of the ideological beliefs and practices of small business owners, cultural boundaries are usually construed as ethnic or class based in origin (Aldrich and Waldinger, 1990; Bonacich and Light, 1988; Butler, 1991; Park, 1997). Despite collective gains, little is known about middle class women making a living outside paid employment and independent of traditional family firms managed by men. The growing acceptance of women in public trading activities and managerial roles should be explored from their perspective, so that the negotiation of commonly held social expectations can be documented. How women narrate their experiences of work, class, motherhood, and political activism can be the basis for valuable sociological knowledge about the ways they negotiate changes in their lives (Biggart 1989; Cockburn 1985; Hill-Collins, 1990; Epstein 1988, 1989, 1990; Ginsberg 1989; Gerson 1985, 1993; Hochschild, 1989; Westwood, 1988).[3] From 1990 through 1993, I conducted over fifty-four interviews with women entrepreneurs, including thirty-five in-depth, life history interviews on the premises of the owner's business, and nineteen unstructured conversation-based interviews at dinner or breakfast meetings. I spoke informally with many people in the local environments in which these small firm owners operated. The main research for this study was conducted with members of The New Jersey Association of

Women Business Owners, an affiliate of the National Association of Women Business Owners. The resources of association participants include shared cultural understandings, knowledge, beliefs, skills and information, as well as modest amounts of capital and access to credit.[4] I attended association meetings in central, northern and southern New Jersey where I observed and interacted with participants.

Women who choose a gender-based association as one of their reference groups reveal many of the challenges and tensions that are involved in changing the sexual status quo in business. A woman must identify herself as an entrepreneur, referring to groups of independent business owners who define and socially establish who a business woman is, how she should act and what her social interests might be. The social establishment of a business first involves the personal identity of the owner and business formed through interaction. Second, social establishment takes place in ethnic, class or professional networks which support the business, both in its market position and in its role in the community. Third, the collective affiliation of similar businesses influences the social establishment of new businesses through the power of associations and industry groups. The sociology of entrepreneurship has focused almost exclusively on the second aspect of social establishment, ethnic, class and professional ties which explain the structural position of categories of small businesses and the relative success of particular ethnic groups.

As late as the 1990's, women could not participate as full members in some of the largest and most influential club-based, voluntary associations which attract small business owners and other executives, including the Elks (1995), the Lion's Clubs, the Masons, and the Rotary Clubs (1989). Women's auxiliary clubs provided a forum for the participation of the wives and relatives of male members. Even though the Chambers of Commerce were open to both sexes, in some states and localities separate "Women's Chambers" increased in the 1970's and 1980's to help women make connections, lobby and achieve stronger leadership roles. While barriers to women's participation in the male dominated small business associations continue to fall, acceptance or resistance to the equal participation of women in small business circles remains rooted in local cultural assumptions about gender roles. My field research helped me to ascertain the business women's definitions of the situations and ideas they encountered. I investigate the reasons women give for their choice of business ownership, the social and material resources they use to sustain their enterprise, how they interpret their employment experience, their use of voluntary associations, the ways in which they organize their responsibilities to their children and households, and their attitudes toward government.

DEFINING AND SELECTING STUDY PARTICIPANTS

What are "women owned businesses?" The Bureau of the Census defines a firm as women-owned if the sole owner or at least half the partners are women. A Corporation is "woman-owned" if 50 percent or more of the shares are owned by women. Federal agencies define a "women-owned business" as 51 percent owned, controlled (exercising authority to make policy decisions), and operated by a woman or women.[5] The approximate, imprecise definitions used by the government are the basis for professional research on small businesses. Business partnerships between husband and wife may still be classified as "woman-owned" if the majority of shares in a firm are held by the wife. I use the term "woman-owned" as a measure of women's market participation, because holding the legal status of an owner is a significant form of power in the management and disposition of property. Consistent with the sociological and dictionary use of the term, in this project entrepreneurship is defined as the risk of capital in the formation of a business venture (Aldrich, 1989; Bonacich, 1972; Bonacich and Light, 1988; Butler, 1991; Cochran, 1968). I chose to interview women who employ other people, either formally or casually, with the purpose of exploring the ways they managed their firms. Small businesses fill niches in the structure of the local economy; such firms adapt to demands in the business environment. Following Aldrich (1979), niches are defined as "distinct combinations of resources and other constraints that are sufficient to support an organizational form." A separate issue is the social definition of success. With an average personal income of forty thousand dollars, the women in NJAWBO who I interviewed were not wealthy, but middle class. "Success" in the small business world is equated with survival and modest growth (Bonacich, 1980; Park, 1997).[6]

OBSERVER IN THE SUBURBS

The position of the interviewer in the setting is important to explaining the interaction between women in the study and the reasons they chose to trust me. While conducting the fieldwork for this study, from 1990 to 1993, I lived in Middlesex County, New Jersey. Middlesex is a densely populated area containing industrial centers such as Edison, Piscataway, New Brunswick, South River, Old Bridge and Woodbridge. In 1992 the population of Middlesex County was 671,780 who occupied 310.6 square miles of land. Although the county hosts suburban housing developments, the landscape is shaped by the scars, infrastructure and architecture of generations of industrial and residential development on major transportation routes such as Route 1 and lower Route 287. It is necessary to drive a car if one needs access to commercial sites in the vicinity of these highways.

My mother and father form a local academic household associated with Rutgers University. They reside in Highland Park, a middle class bedroom community sitting on a clay hill above the Raritan River across from New Brunswick. The identities of "daughter" and "graduate student" gave me legitimacy when I approached the NJAWBO Middlesex Chapter. The members accepted me as a native of their world. Many of the women I met pursued higher education while they held jobs in the private economy. I did not own a small business. Thus, I lacked authority about the operation and management of small firms, but the women in NJAWBO defined me as a potential owner. I was asked at every event when I would open my own business and what ideas I had for independent business projects. They suggested that social scientists can sell information, writing, public relations, and marketing research services. I was encouraged to imagine ways to turn my education and occupational experiences into forms of commodity. Like the women I interviewed, I could use my resources to establish myself as a middleman business owner or a specialty niche trader, service provider or light manufacturer. This might create a more secure economic position for myself than that of adjunct instructor or temporary worker. The members of the association helped me to imagine a fictive self with the identity of a potential entrepreneur in order to participate in their network. The processes of forming an entrepreneurial identity and transforming knowledge and experience into commodities defined by the business women, revealed to me the disjuncture between market ideology as it shapes a public position for the woman entrepreneur as a capitalist, and the beliefs of the association members that anyone, even a penniless graduate student, could refer to herself as a business owner by adopting the entrepreneurial narrative and working to make the aspiration a reality. Their booster spirit toward my project and my ambition was affirming, but at times their conviction in their own market solutions redefined my role. They listed me in their directory as a business consultant.

As I lived and worked in the suburban environment, my understanding of the organization of resources and social class references deepened. I began to consider how my own situation could be related to the narratives of the women owners. We shared some things in common. First, financial uncertainty was modified by the recognition that I possessed resources, including my family support and graduate training. Second, I shared a dream of social mobility or class stability without the domination of direct supervision in wage or salaried employment. Third, as every middle class person who negotiates market agreements, from the car loan, lease or mortgage, to the price of a ticket out of town, I had knowledge of some business practices. Class and cultural experience create forms of social knowledge that can be applied to new situations.

Suburban life is organized around sites of consumption, supermarkets, malls, and downtown shopping districts in old town centers. Whether shopping for a house, car, personal service or mall sale bargain, the ability to interpret and negotiate resources as monetary or cash equivalents in exchange relationships is a fundamental social skill that any suburbanite must practice. Middle class adulthood is sustained by many small calculations, of credit, interest, mortgage, and other measures of abstract value related to purchases and consumption patterns. How one manages these calculations is also a measure of success.

When a chapter officer offered me a ride to a local meeting, she arrived in a recently purchased, four door Mazda sedan with white leather interior. Our entire conversation consisted of a tour of the vehicle's features, including a mobile phone. She could talk to a speaker in the car cabin while driving through traffic on the highway. Although it was expensive, she felt that she had earned it, and she was showing off one of the spoils of her good credit rating. Significant amounts of time during her working day are spent driving around the state visiting clients and potential leads, people doing small jobs for her projects, and attending business association and Chamber of Commerce meetings. The automobile is a work site, and its comforts and limitations are intimate features of doing business. New technologies make it possible for individuals to do business on the road or on the sidewalk, but the women I spoke with valued their separate office spaces and sometimes the privacy of their cars as sites in which work and the presentation of self could be organized (Goffman, 1959). Technology and structural changes in the economy reflexively condition cultural practices, but do not determine them. Business women develop social roles and refer their identities and practices to existing groups based on shared experiences.

THE ORIGINS OF SOCIAL ESTABLISHMENT

Theories of identity and group processes are at the center of the relationship between sociological and psychological theory. William James' (1890) theory of the "social self" accounted for the formation of potential selves or identities through the individual's references to various social groups and individuals. A woman has as many selves as there are groups to which she seeks to belong. Charles Horton Cooley (1902) wrote that a "self-concept" developed through an internal dialogue in which the individual imagined how others would interpret and interact in a situation. According to Cooley, the individual developed a selective affinity to groups outside of his or her immediate social environment based on social imagination. The individual and the groups in which he or she participates, continuously remake each other in an ongoing process of communication and change.[7] George Herbert Mead (1934) claimed that the genesis of the self is in our ability to play the parts of others and to respond to our own role playing. Mead's "self" develops through multiple roles into a generalized other, assimilating reality to its own needs, and thus establishing a regular pattern through the process of adjusting to the social world. Embedded in these theories is the argument that by referring to others, groups teach us how to organize our self emotions and social expectations as well as our practices.

Robert K. Merton criticized Mead for failing to offer a systematic, empirical analysis of the structural conditions under which the individual selects and orients the self to out-groups, or those to which he or she is not a member.[8] Merton (1950, 1957) synthesized social psychological "reference group theory" with sociological theory by looking for the limited range of structural conditions that would explain individual choices of reference groups.[9] Explanations of individual behavior are systematized in relation to "the values or standards of other individuals and groups as a ...frame of reference" (Merton and Kitt, 1950).[10] Reference group theory offers "middle range" explanations for individual and group behavior, by focusing on the ways individuals relate their identities to particular groups in order to pursue goals such as normative values of success. The historical development of particular professional roles and statuses can also create new reference groups. Thus in 1965 it would have been unusual for an ordinary working woman to say that she was planning to become an entrepreneur, but by 1985 such a claim would have been common.

The insight that individuals orient themselves to groups outside their familiar frame of reference in shaping their behavior and evaluation helps to explain the formation of entrepreneurial selves by middle class suburban women who have established prior work histories as employees, but little experience as independent deal makers. I argue that women's entrepreneurship develops in relationship to the groups women participate in and refer to in forming entrepreneurial identities. This allows us to examine entrepreneurship in cultural context without attributing universal motives, values or psychologies to business women. Through a business association, the woman business owner can relate to reference groups of entrepreneurs and capitalists who shape the public definitions of who belongs in their company and how shared group interests are defined. The individual may only be aspiring to the role of entrepreneur, or having achieved independent firm ownership, she may aspire to a higher economic and social class status than the one to which she belongs.

A COMPARISON OF CLASSICAL THEORETICAL FRAMEWORKS

From European Protestants in the sixteenth and seventeenth centuries (Weber, 1925), to Asian families in twentieth century North America (Bonacich and Model, 1981; Park, 1997), the sociology of entrepreneurship argues that business formation is a response to social disadvantage, economic insecurity or structural stresses, which push individuals in subordinate ethnic, racial, class or gender groups to risk small amounts of capital in the formation of firms in niches that are undesirable by dominant classes. By generating capital through small enterprise, the group improves its collective status, even rising to dominate other groups in society. Contrary to theories that posit stress or displacement as causes of women's entrepreneurship, I argue that cultural beliefs are among the resources that condition the development of entrepreneurial identities in historical and structural contexts.

WEBER: BELIEFS VERSUS RATIONALIZING FORCES

In his classic study of Christian entrepreneurship, *The Protestant Ethic and the Spirit of Capitalism* (1930), Max Weber argued that cultural values and ideas act as guides for action when people organize their economic activities (Weber, [1905], 1989; Swidler, 1986). Early Calvinist ideas emphasized asceticism and self discipline. Weber connected the spirit of modern, rationalizing capitalism, to the influence of secularized Protestant belief systems, communicated through the works of writers and intellectuals, among them Benjamin Franklin, a patriot of the American revolution. Weber wrote that class situation is ultimately market situation (Weber, 1978).[11] Entrepreneurship is an economic strategy which maintains household stability in the face of hostile economic and social limitations. The latent effects of capitalist, market based strategies are changes in status order or class formation, as in the case of the rise of the protestant entrepreneurs.

Theories about business formation that emphasize individual virtue, thrift, and the just returns of hard work are characteristic middle class American standards. From Benjamin Franklin's *Autobiography* (1722) and *Poor Richard's Almanac* (1733), to Horatio Alger's *Ragged Dick* (1868) to Sam Walton's *Made in America: My Story* (1992), American biography and fiction emphasize the individual's triumph over the status barriers of poverty and class through the pursuit of self-interest in the market.[12] These popular works appeal to individual aspirations for social equality and mobility.

While gender does not appear as a separate theme in Weber, we can account for women's entrepreneurship by studying the expansion of their participation in market processes over time. In Weber's theory, human action is guided by belief systems which develop as cultures increasingly base their organization on rational principles rather than customs. According to Weber "market freedom," the range of economic action and the degree of autonomy allowed to individuals in market relationships, is limited by "market regulation," which includes tradition and convention, as well as law.[13] Women and men still hold beliefs about gender roles that regulate their behaviors, whether women are challenging the traditional male bastions of voluntary leadership in business associations or "fitting in" to cultural expectations about femininity in business dealings. Weber defined business credit as "that credit which is extended to take up as a means of increasing control over the requisites of profit making activity."[14] Tradition and convention created boundaries that have limited women's access to independent control of credit, property and trade. When individuals hold traditional gender role expectations that men must lead and women follow, they impede negotiation and the communication of terms. The rationalization of contemporary gender roles involves overcoming those aspects of male and female roles which impede doing business as well as other forms of information sharing. The "economic action" of women, their peaceful attempts to control resources for economic ends, can therefore be described as culturally bounded by gender conventions which are contested by actors in the liberal polity.

LESSONS FROM THE ETHNIC PARADIGM

Studies of ethnic entrepreneurship which appeared in the 1970's and 1980's argued that oppressed minority and immigrant groups form entrepreneurial businesses as a strategy to build social and economic status (Light, 1972; Bonacich, 1972; Light and Bonacich, 1988; Bonacich and Modell, 1978; Portes and Bach, 1985; Westwood, 1988). When an ethnic group encounters blocked opportunities for participation and integration in the economy and society, individual members of the group find opportunities for small business ownership and create innovations in existing distribution networks. These studies find that immigrant and minority entrepreneur communities function as either middlemen, providing goods and trade services between the large producers and corporations and the masses of consumers in local markets of the economy, or as the backbone of an ethnic economy composed of group members. Entrepreneurial activities allow a group to avoid the potentially negative consequences of their social subordination, stabilize the economic basis for their community, and build networks of mutual aid and reciprocal exchange (Bonacich and Modell, 1980; Bonacich and Light, 1989; Butler, 1991). The distribution of resources by gender is not a separate theme in this literature; it is subsumed by discussions of cultural adaptation and social reproduction by the "ethnic" status group. Although the gender subordination of women, and middle man minority theory, may appear incongruous, Patricia Greene argues that the middleman position of independent women business owners is a legacy of the gender segregation of the work place (Greene and Johnson, 1995).[15] Women are positioned as a group of outsiders in business ownership, who are forced to assume a functional position in market niches that are less desirable to members of the dominant group, white males.

RESOURCE-DEPENDENCY AND ETHNIC RESOURCES

Another way of understanding the ethnic paradigm is the resource-dependence model. Based on extensive studies of Asian immigrant communities, Ivan Light argues that immigrant entrepreneurship is explained by the group's access to resources (Light, 1984; Light and Bonacich, 1991).[16] Ethnic resources are shared cultural understandings and institutions, the "social features" of groups, including values, beliefs, knowledge, skills, information, and customs. Class resources are cultural and material accumulations, including private property, wealth, and investments in human capital.

MARXIST VISIONS OF DE-VALUED LABOR

In the Marxist perspective the expansion of small business classes occurs because of large scale economic structural changes beyond the control of individuals. Structural conditions in the economy serve as constraints on the kind of social action possible in a given epoch. Women are dominated in a set of impersonal structural conditions that reinforce their class subordination (Engels, 1884). In the "Theory of Concentration and Expropriation" in Volume One of *Das Kapital*,[17] Karl Marx argued that the concentration of production and capital investment in large scale capitalist enterprises cheapens labor as a commodity and drives small scale producers out of the market. Large scale industry accelerates the expropriation of the surplus value of labor. The appearance of small producers would logically indicate that large businesses are subcontracting in order to lower their labor costs. A shrinking number of white collar jobs and lower level positions combine with deindustrialization in the economy to create downsizing and subcontracting patterns (Beechey, 1987; Glassford, 1990; Harvey, 1989; Pollert, 1988; Piore and Sable, 1984; Piore, 1988; Rubery, 1989; Steinmetz and Wright, 1989, Wright, 1985).[18] By employing individuals performing clerical, service, or administrative support work in small firms, business owners organize the bottom of the labor market for the benefit of a power structure that is undergoing a period of transformation in the social relations of production.

NETWORKING AND THE EVOLUTION OF BUSINESS

Howard Aldrich (1989) argues that we need to imagine "women entrepreneurs as embedded in a social context, channeled and facilitated, or constrained and inhibited, by their position in social networks."[19] Aldrich proposes three key life events which shape the networks women entrepreneurs enter into or construct: the work place, marriage and family, and organized social life. Aldrich does not assume that family networks are intact "ethnic" networks. Women's networks reflect how the social organization of the culture is shaped by gender, but he is the first to test common assumptions about the causality of women's entrepreneurship. Aldrich and a team of researchers report that women do not have different networking behaviors than those of men, a common assumption among journalists and women themselves.[20] Women's businesses fill niches in markets, providing goods and services in ways that adapt to the environment. Karyn Loscocco, arguing from a leftist feminist perspective, proves that men and women are clustered in different kinds of business niches; thus women are structurally subordinate to men as a collective group in the small business economy (Loscocco, 1990).

I view the structural changes in the economy that produced increases in self-employment and small business formation, not as a limitation on individual careers, but as new conditions for adaptation by individuals in the managerial middle classes. The expansion of service industries created new incentives or opportunities for business formation. Women's entrepreneurship may reflect increased opportunities for economic action independent of the social control of the family or corporation, not a response to collective limitation. Middle-class women in the predominantly white "mainstream" of America learn how to do business by living and working in environments in which exchange and value are socially negotiated, and entrepreneurial strategies are touted as solutions to social and economic limitations.

CHAPTER NOTES

1. U.S. Department of Commerce, *1992 Economic Census of Women Owned Businesses* (Washington, D.C.: U.S. Government Printing Office), p. 2.

2. U.S. Small Business Administration, Office of Advocacy. "Facts About Small Business." [1996] http://www.sba.gov/ADVO/stats/fact1.html [January 26, 1998].

3. Nicole Woolsey Biggart, *Charismatic Capitalism: Direct Selling Organizations in America* (Chicago: University of Chicago Press, 1989); Cynthia Cockburn, *Machinery of Dominance* (London: Pluto Press, 1985); Cynthia Fuchs Epstein, *Deceptive Distinctions: Sex, Gender and the Social Order* (New Haven: Yale University Press, 1988), and "Tinker bells and Pinups: The Construction and Reconstruction of Gender Boundaries at Work." In M. Lamont and M. Fournier (eds.) *Cultivating Differences: Symbolic Boundaries and the Making of Inequality* (Chicago: University of Chicago Press, 1992); Faye Ginsberg, *Contested Lives* (Berkeley: University of California Press, 1989); Kathleen Gerson, *Hard Choices: How Women Decide About Work, Career and Motherhood* (Berkeley: University of California Press, 1985); Arlie Hochschild, *The Second Shift* (New York: Viking, 1989); Sallie Westwood and Parminder Bhachu (eds.) *Enterprising Women: Ethnicity, Economy and Gender Relations* (NY: Routledge, 1988).

4. Ivan Light and Edna Bonacich, *Immigrant Entrepreneurs: Koreans in Los Angeles 1965-1982* (Berkeley: University of California Press, 1991), pp. 18-19.

5. U.S. Department of Commerce, *Women and Business Ownership: An Annotated Bibliography* (Washington, D. C.: U. S. Government Printing Office, July, 1986), p. 7.

6. Kyeyoung Park, *The Korean American Dream* (New York: Cornell University Press, 1997) p. 204.

7. Walton H. Hamilton, "Cooley, Charles Horton," in Edwin R.A. Seligman, ed. *Encyclopedia of the Social Sciences* (New York: The Macmillan Company, 1931) pp. 355-356.

8. Robert K. Merton, *Social Theory and Social Structure* (New York: The Free Press, 1957), pp. 238-239.

9. The first three theorists to establish the term "reference group theory" were social psychologists Herbert Hyman (1942), who developed a psychology of status, Theodore M. Newcomb (1943), whose study of Bennington students explored how they related themselves to the college as a community, and Samuel Stouffer who theorized the concept of "relative deprivation" in his study of *The American Soldier* (1949), to capture how men evaluated their conditions based on a relative comparison to other groups. In the 1940's Hyman, Newcomb and Stouffer were contemporaries of Robert K. Merton. See, Herbert H. Hyman, "Reference Groups," in David L. Sills (ed.) *International Encyclopedia of the Social Sciences, Vol. 13* (New York: The Macmillan Co. & Free Press, 1968) pp. 353-359.

10. Robert K. Merton and Alice S. Kitt, "Contributions to the Theory of Reference Group Behavior," in Robert K. Merton and Paul Lazarsfeld (eds.), *Continuities in Social Research: Studies in the Scope and Method of the American Soldier* (Glencoe, IL: The Free Press, 1950), pp. 40-105.

11. Max Weber, *Economy and Society, Volume Two* (Berkeley: University of California Press), p. 928.

12. Charles Gregory, "Horatio Alger, Jr. 1832-99" pp.7-8 in Justin Wintle, (ed.) *Makers of Nineteenth Century Culture: 1800-1914*, (Boston: Routledge & Kegan Paul, 1982). "To repeat a famous quotation from Alger's publisher A.K. Loring, "you can hear the cry of triumph of the oppressed over the oppressor."

13. Max Weber, *Economy and Society, Volume 1*, Guenther Roth and Claus Wittich (eds.) (Berkeley: University of California Press, 1978), p. 82.

14. Max Weber, *Economy and Society Volume 1*, Guenther Roth and Claus Wittich (eds.) (Berkeley: University of California Press, 1978), p. 91.

15. Patricia G. Greene and Margaret A. Johnson, "Social Learning and Middleman Minority Theory: Explanations for Self-Employed Women," *The National Journal of Sociology*, (Draft, Summer 1995).

16. Ivan Light, "Immigrant and Ethnic Enterprise in North America," *Ethnic and Racial Studies* (7) (1984), pp.195-216; Light and Bonacich, *Immigrant Entrepreneurs: Koreans in Los Angeles 1965-1982* (Berkeley: University of California Press, 1991), pp.18-19.

17. Karl Marx, *Capital: A Critical Analysis of Capitalist Production Volume I* (New York: International Publishers, 1965), Ch. XXV, section 2.

18. Margaret Glassford, "The State and Liberal Feminism," American Sociological Association, 1991; David Harvey, *The Condition of Postmodernity* (London: Basil Blackwell, 1989); Michael J. Piore and Charles Sable, *The Second Industrial Divide* (New York: Basic Books, 1984); Michael J. Piore, "The Changing Role of Small Business in the U.S. Economy," Institute of Labor Studies, ILO, 1988; Jill Rubery, "Labor Market Flexibility in Britain," in Green, F. (ed.), *Restructuring the British Economy* (UK: Harvester-Wheatsheaf, 1989); George Steinmetz and Erik Olin Wright, "The Rise and Fall of the Petty Bourgeoisie: Changing Patterns of Self-Employment in the Postwar United States," *American Journal of Sociology* 13(1989): 273-305.

19. Howard Aldrich, "Networking Among Women Entrepreneurs." In Oliver Hagan, Carol Rivchun, and Donald Sexton (eds.) *Women Owned Businesses* (New York: Praeger, 1989), p. 104.

20. Howard E. Aldrich and Amanda Elam Brickman, "Strong Ties, Weak Ties, and Strangers: Do Women Differ from Men in Their Use of Networking to Obtain Assistance?" Draft, University of North Carolina at Chapel Hill, 1995.

Structural Conditions: Women Owned Businesses in the U.S.

Changes in the global and domestic economy over the last three decades facilitated the expansion of service industries, and created the conditions for a rapid increase in the small business sectors in the United States (Acs, 1998). Piore and Sabel (1984) argue that it was impossible for the U.S. economy to maintain stability in markets based on industrial mass production, so self-employment and entrepreneurship in service industries took on increasing importance in reorganizing employment during restructuring and downsizing.[1] Between 1990 and 1996, the number of corporations and partnerships increased from five million to seven million firms. The number of sole proprietorships increased from fifteen million to seventeen million firms. This is an increase of 3% annually.[2] Small businesses account for 47% of all sales in the country, and roughly half the gross domestic product (SBA, 1996). From 1976 to 1990, small firms with less than 500 employees provided 53% of total employment and 65% of net new jobs. The political and sociological meanings that are attached to entrepreneurship and self-employment by government, associations and other interests such as corporations develop in the context of these historical changes and structural conditions.

Market position, or control over resources, defines economic class position in a capitalist economy. Thus, the organization of markets and the organization of status in society are closely related (Weber, 1978). The Office of Advocacy of the Small Business Administration in the U. S. defines small business firms with less than 500 employees or sole proprietorships with less than 100 employees, as a primary vehicle of social integration in the new economy, quote:

> Small business is the vehicle by which millions access the American Dream
> by creating opportunities for women, minorities and immigrants. In this
> evolutionary process, community plays the crucial and indispensable role

of providing the social glue and networking that binds small firms together in both high tech and "Main Street" activities.[3]

The perception that small business has a "social glue" function has become a rationale for government policy and political strategy, as well as business association lobbies. But is this perception correct? What can structural patterns in types of ownership, distribution by industry and percentage employed tell us about the integration of women into business?

The National Foundation for Women Business Owners claims that women owners have more employees than the Fortune 500 companies. The group issued a widely reported press release on April 5, 1995, with the dramatic headline, "Women-Owned Businesses Out-pace All U.S. Firms." The text reports:

> Women owned businesses now employ 35 percent more people in the U.S. than the Fortune 500 companies employ worldwide, according to a national study by the National Foundation for Women Business Owners (NFWBO) and Dun & Bradstreet Information Services (DBIS).[4]
> ....reports that women-owned businesses now number 7.7 million, provide jobs for 15.5 million people and generate nearly $1.4 trillion in sales, according to NFWBO's and DBIS's latest estimates.

This implies that women are major players in building and supporting employment in the United States. Although women firm owners are of great importance, the argument by NFWBO that their contribution to employment and economic growth is equal or even superior to the majority of small businesses owned by men or to the companies of the Fortune 500 misrepresents the situation of women in business. They divert public attention away from ongoing patterns of gender clustering, segregation, and their limited access to capital and business credit.

First, the figures reported by the National Foundation for Women Business Owners include both self-employed individuals and owners who employ workers in small firms. According to the 1992 Census, women own 6 million businesses, 35% of the 15 million small businesses in the United States, and contribute $643 billion dollars to the economy, or 19% of all firm receipts (U.S. Department of Commerce, 1992). But to place women's contribution in perspective, it is important to note that self-employment accounts for only 8% of workers in the United States today, 9% of men and 6% of women (U.S. Department of Labor, 1996). Few of the self-employed employ anyone else. Three quarters of small business owners are employed in a wage and salary job when they start a new business (SBA, 1996).[5]

While the number of women owned firms continues to rise, most of the increase in women's share of U.S. business ownership is attributable to the increase in sole proprietorships which employ no one. The small number of employers is illustrated in Table 1.

TABLE 1. U.S. WOMEN SOLE PROPRIETORSHIP EMPLOYERS

Year	# WOBusiness	# Employers	% Employers
1982	2,612,621	311,662	11.9
1987	4,114,787	618,198	15.0
1992	5888883	817,773	13.9 (-2.9)
Cum.% U.S.	34% of U.S.	26% of U.S.	+2% Change

Source: U.S. Dept. of Commerce 1987 ,1992.
Total Number of Small Businesses in 1992 = 17,253,143.[6]

Census and federal reports show that the percentage of women-owned businesses that employ people on a regular basis only increased two percent over a ten year period from 1982 to 1992. The number of sole proprietorships and partnerships regularly employing others and managed on a continuous basis by women, moderately increased to 15% in 1987 before dropping to 14% in 1992. The reported aggregate statistics since 1982 include a drop in the percentage. Overall, this is a pattern of stability within a larger pattern of structural change in the economy of the United States. The number of firms and employers doubled, but the percentage of employers relative to the total number of businesses did not increase rapidly. With new technologies giving individuals access to knowledge, communications and trade at a rapidly expanding pace, self-employment will out pace the formation of firms with employees. Women's self-employment should continue to rise within this trend, but their relative share of ownership of firms employing workers may not increase in equal measure.

In New Jersey, the state in which the field research for this project was conducted, we find modest gains in the percentage of women employers. By the most conservative estimate of employer firms in New Jersey, the number of entrepreneurial businesses owned by women more than doubled in five years. In 1982 the U.S. Census counted 63,243 women owned firms, including 8,997 regular employers in the state of New Jersey. In 1987 the count was 117,373 firms, including 19,389 regular employers.[7] In 1987 businesses with regular employees in New Jersey were 16.5% of the total number of women owned businesses, up from 14% in 1982. In 1992 there were 164,798 firms, including 26,062 employers.[8] The percentage of employers relative to the total number of small businesses declined slightly between 1987 and 1992. The cumulative increase in the percentage of employers was only 1.6%. While the numbers of self-employed proprietorships have more than doubled, the percentage of employers only increased 2% over a decade.[9] Employers generate 85% of receipts or profits. If the percentage share of women-owned firms employing others continues to increase by only 2 to 3 percent every ten years, it is questionable whether or not the percentage of women who are regular employers will equal the proportional share of all such firms owned by men during the next half century.

The claim that women-owned businesses employ more people in the U.S. than the Fortune 500 companies combined employ worldwide, can be called into question if we examine regular corporations. In compliance with the Women's Business Ownership Act of 1988, a survey of "C" corporations is included in the summary of the 1992 *Economic Census of Women Owned Businesses*. The *Fortune 500 Index* is a status index of the largest firms in the United States. It is the creation of a commercial magazine designed for readers who are interested in following business trends. The firms in the Fortune 500 Index are corporations selected from a national survey in 1992 of over two million (2,033,369) firms. In the *1992 Census of Women Owned Businesses*, we discover that women employed 11% of the employees of C corporations. Men continued to employ 89% of all employees in this form of business organization.

To distinguish types of businesses, three forms of organization are included in the Small Business Administration and U.S. Department of Commerce statistics: (1) sole proprietorships or unincorporated businesses owned by an individual, (2) partnerships which are unincorporated, and (3) Subchapter S corporations, businesses with fewer than thirty-five stock holders who elect to be taxed once through the income of individual owners rather than as regular corporations.[10] "C" corporations are called 'regular corporations' because they exist as legal entities separate from the individual liability of the owners. The omission of regular C corporations from past Department of Commerce census reports has led to confusion over reporting the total number of women owned businesses in the United States.[11] If six and a half million women sole proprietors are compared to 500 large corporations, the comparison between different categories of business type is misleading.

If we compare the percentage of women-owned C corporations in each industry to the percentage of receipts they contribute in that industry, the productivity or profitability of women-owned firms in 1992 appears to be low, indicating smaller or less efficient businesses. This is illustrated in Table 2. Women own roughly a quarter of American "C" corporations. This is progress compared to the past, but they account for under 15% of receipts in each industry category. The exception is agriculture, a traditional family business in which female headed incorporation may facilitate loan applications.

Women are a minority in the ownership of sole proprietorships, including those firms with employees. In 1992, women owned 33% of sole proprietorships and men owned 63%.[13] Furthermore, women owned businesses are clustered in services, retail and wholesale trade. Forty-one percent (41%) of all service and retail businesses in the country are owned by women, and 64% of receipts from women-owned firms are generated from

TABLE 2. PERCENT OF WOMEN-OWNED C CORP & RECEIPTS[12]

INDUSTRY IN 1992	%WOMEN'S C	%RECEIPTS
WOMEN'S TOTAL	26%	9%
AGRICULTURE	26%	20%
MINING	22%	4%
CONSTRUCTION	25%	15%
MANUFACTURING	23%	7%
TRANSPORTATION	29%	10%
WHOLESALE	25%	13%
RETAIL	31%	9%
FINANCE	24%	8%
SERVICES	24%	8%
OTHER	20%	4%

U.S. Department of Commerce, 1992. Total # of C Corporations = 2,033,369; women's share was 517,832. Receipts are for companies with paid employees ($1,000,000); the total for all C corporations was $10,747,083. and women's share was $931,606.

retail trade, services and wholesale trade (U.S. Department of Commerce, 1992). Women owned businesses have shown twice the percentage increase of all small businesses (SBA 1996).[14] According to the Bureau of the Census, the number of non-farm sole proprietorships owned by women increased 58% between 1982 and 1987, from 2,612,621 to 4,114,787.[15] In 1992, the United States Census Bureau reported six million firms other than C corporations, and six and a half million firms owned by women if such regular corporations are included, employing thirteen million people.[16] This is a 43% increase nationwide between 1987 and 1992, or over 100% since 1982. In contrast, the increase in all small businesses has been 49% since 1982. But sole proprietorships are the smallest and most economically vulnerable organizations; both capitalization and liability are the responsibility of the owner.

EMPLOYMENT DISTRIBUTION AS A MIRROR OF THE ECONOMY

According to the United States Small Business Administration, women-owned businesses employ one out of every five workers or 18.5 million employees.[17] When businesses owned by women are examined as a separate category among small employers (sole proprietorships, partnerships, and S Corporations), we see: (1) the predominance of retail and business service firms, and (2) that this pattern mirrors the stratification of small business

TABLE 3. EMPLOYMENT % BY INDUSTRY, 1992

INDUSTRY IN 1992	US EMPLOY % DISTRIBUTION	WOMEN'S EMPLOY %
TOTAL	ALL	23%
AGRICULTURE	1%	1%
MINING	1%	1%
CONSTRUCTION	8%	6%
MANUFACTURING	14%	13%
TRANSPORTATION	4%	5%
WHOLESALE	6%	6%
RETAIL	25%	30%
FINANCE	6%	5%
SERVICES	34%	34%
OTHER	19%	15%

Calculated from U.S. Department of Commerce, 1992. Total employment in U.S. small businesses = 27,403,974 in 17,253,142 firms, including sole proprietorships, partnerships and subchapter S corporations. Women's share is 5,888,883 firms with 6,252,029. employees.[18]

firms regardless of the owner's gender.

The majority of employees of small businesses are in services and retail trade, the two modal categories of business ownership for women. These categories of business are comprised of many small firms with redundant products and services, competing to survive at the local levels of the economy. The patterns of employment associated with women owned businesses approach the percentage distribution of small business employment by all firms in the United States.

Women owned C corporations have a much lower percentage of employees than their reported percentage of corporate ownership. This is illustrated in Table 4. Some of the factors that explain women clustering in small firms with fewer employees include low capitalization, less time in industry, their lower number of work hours, and constraints on their access to commercial credit.[20] Men may also form small corporations which employ few workers, but because we deal in collective categories a few successful men represent their entire sex. Nonetheless, the patterns I have discussed confirm that strong economic and cultural boundaries privileging male ownership and management of human and capital resources still dominate the economy.

While small businesses are increasing in importance as sources of employment, high risks and uncertainty are attached to small firm management. According to the Small Business Administration, Dun and

TABLE 4. WOMEN'S C CORP % EMPLOYMENT [19]

INDUSTRY IN 1992	% WOMEN'S C	% EMPLOY
TOTAL	26%	11%
AGRICULTURE	26%	17%
MINING	22%	07%
CONSTRUCTION	25%	16%
MANUFACTURING	23%	09%
TRANSPORTATION	29%	14%
WHOLESALE	25%	20%
RETAIL	31%	09%
FINANCE	24%	08%
SERVICES	24%	14%
OTHER	20%	04%

U.S. Department of Commerce, 1992. N of companies with paid employees=1,656,575; women's share was 426,681. N of employees=62,951,041; women's share=6,965,037.

Bradstreet Corporation, and the Administrative Office of the U.S. Courts, the percentage of all firms dissolved for both voluntary and involuntary reasons is 53% after four years, 62% after six years, and 71% after eight years.[21] Rather than providing lasting, long term employment in an individual's career, small firm employment may be short term, as firms open and close more frequently, and low wages and benefits increase the likelihood of turnover among workers seeking a better wage bargain (Hodson and Sullivan, 1998).[22] Small firms with under 500 workers also undergo mergers, restructuring, and downsizing, making growth in the number of "permanent employees" sensitive to business conditions.

Suburban association members may be even more prone to represent services that depend on the strength of other businesses. Membership categories of business with more than twenty members listed in the November 11, 1995 New Jersey Association of Women Business

Owners Membership Roster include:

40> LISTINGS

Financial Planning	48
Marketing	47
Consultants	45
Educational Services	45
Accountants	44
Management Consults	41
Computer Consults	40

30> LISTINGS

Business Services	38
Health Care	38
Graphic Arts/Design	34
Attorneys	33
Legal Services	30

20> LISTINGS

Desktop Publishing	29
Advertising	26
Interior Design	25
Real Estate	24
Printers	23
Tax Services	22
Construction	21
Bookkeeping	20
Public Relations	20
Travel and Tourism	20

<20 SELECT LISTINGS

Distributors	17
Manufacturing	13
Wholesale	12

As one can see, distributors, manufacturers and wholesalers, three of the most lucrative niches in small business ownership, are not the dominant categories of firm ownership among women in the business association directory. Women with managerial and professional experience may be moving out of corporate employment, and thus out of the pipeline for further promotion at the upper levels of management. The knowledge and experiences they have achieved must be adapted to function in smaller scale organizations. The service niches of the economy are crowded with small firms and self-employed individuals. Women, like other small firm owners, face very competitive conditions.

The assertions in the popular press that women employ more workers than the Fortune 500 has social ramifications. First, it misleads the public into believing that women no longer face individual and institutional challenges and inequalities in the business world. Second, people expect women to resolve their own disadvantages by choosing entrepreneurial market strategies. Journalists and women's association spokespersons presumably support women's leadership in business. But the impact of the selective presentation of data about commerce encourages the public to pretend that women are winning a dominant share of the economic pie and therefore suffer no gender-related inequalities. More individual women must break the size and income boundaries that are limiting women's collective place in the structure of business. Women are employing people in increasing percentages. They are part of a general and rapid expansion in small businesses in the new entrepreneurial economy, but women entrepreneurs still play a small role.

CHAPTER NOTES

1. Michael J. Piore and Charles F. Sabel, *The Second Industrial Divide* (New York: Basic Books, 1984), pp. 251-280.

2. Small Business Administration. Office of Advocacy. "Small Businesses in the New Economy." P. 4. http://www.sba.gov/ADVO/stats/ evol_pap.html#Innov [July, 31, 1998].

3. Small Business Administration. Office of Advocacy. "Small Businesses in the New Economy." P. 1. http://www.sba.gov/ADVO/stats/ evol_pap.html#Innov [July, 31, 1998].

4. National Foundation for Women Business Owners, *Women-Owned Businesses: Breaking the Boundaries, The Progress and Achievement of Women-Owned Enterprises* (Silver Spring, MD: NFWBO, 1995).

5. United States Small Business Administration. Office of Advocacy. "Facts About Small Business." [1996] http://www.sba.gov/ADVO/stats/fact1.html [January 26, 1998].

6. U.S. Dept. of Commerce, Bureau of the Censuses, *1987 Economic census of Women Owned Businesses*, and *1992 Economic Census of Women Owned Businesses* (Washington, D.C.: U.S. Government), Table 10, p. 177.

7. United States Department of Commerce, *1987 Census of Women Owned Businesses* (Washington, D.C.: U.S. Government Printing Office), p. 8.

8. United States Department of Commerce, *1992 Economic Census of Women Owned Businesses* (Washington, D.C.: U.S. Government Printing Office), Table 2, p. 12.

9. United States Department of Commerce, *1987 Economic Census of Women Owned Businesses* (Washington, D.C.: U.S. Government Printing Office), Table 2, p. 8.

10. Firms are organizations which employ someone beside the owner. "C" corporations are organizations which usually have more than 100 employees and more than 35 stockholders.

11. C corporations are not counted in the Census tables from 1972 to 1987, but a separate summary table is included in the *1992 Census of Women Owned Businesses*.

12. U.S. Department of Commerce, *1992 Economic Census of Women Owned Businesses* (Washington, D.C.: U.S. Government), p. 3. Total # of C Corporations = 2,033,369; women's share was 517,832. Receipts are for companies with paid employees ($1,000,000); the total for all C corporations was $10,747,083. and women's share was $931,606. ALL=All Industries, AGRI=Agricultural services, forestry, fishing, MINE=Mining, TRS=Transportation and public utilities, WH=Wholesale trade, RET=Retail trade, FIN=Finance, insurance, and real estate, SER=Services, N/C=Industries not classified.

13. National Foundation for Women Business Owners, *A Compendium of National Statistics on Women-Owned Businesses in the U.S.* (Silver Spring, MD: NFWBO, 1994), p. 1-21.

14. United States Small Business Administration. Office of Advocacy. "Facts

About Small Business." [1996] http://www.sba.gov/ADVO/stats/fact1.html [January 26, 1998].

15. United States Small Business Administration, *The State of Small Business: A Report to the President* (Washington: U.S. Printing Office, 1982).

16. United States Small Business Administration, "Small Business Answer Card," Web Page, SBA Office of Advocacy (Washington, D.C. 1995), p. 2.

17. Small Business Administration Web Page, "Statistics on Women Business Ownership," July 8, 1997, p.1.

18. Calculated from U.S. Department of Commerce, *1992 Economic Census of Women Owned Businesses* (Washington, D.C.: U.S. Government Printing Office), p. 13 and 177. Total employment in U.S. small businesses = 27,403,974 in 17,253,142 firms, including sole proprietorships, partnerships and subchapter S corporations. Women's share is 5,888,883 firms with 6,252,029. employees.

19. U.S. Department of Commerce, *1992 Economic Census of Women Owned Businesses* (Washington, D.C.: U.S. Government Printing Office), p. 3. N of companies with paid employees=1,656,575; women's share was 426,681. N of employees=62,951,041; women's share=6,965,037. ALL=AllIndustries, AGRI=Agricultural services, forestry, fishing, MINE=Mining, TRS=Transportation and public utilities, WH=Wholesale trade, RET=Retail trade, FIN=Finance, insurance, and real estate, SER=Services, N/C=Industries not classified.

20. Richard Joseph Boden, *Gender Differences in Entrepreneurial Selection and Performance*, Dissertation, University of Maryland, 1990.

21. United States Small Business Administration. Office of Advocacy. "Small Business Answer Card 1997." [1997] http://www.sba.gov/ADVO/stats/answer.html [January 26, 1998].

22. Randy Hodson and Teresa Sullivan, *The Social Organization of Work, 2nd Edition* (Wadsworth Publishing Company, 1995), pp.409-410.

CHAPTER THREE:
Work Experiences as Knowledge and Motivation

The evidence that emerges from sociological studies of women business owners shows that their former employment formed the basis of their knowledge and confidence to open an independent business (Aldrich, Reese, Dubini, 1989; Loscocco and Robinson et al, 1991).[1] However, not only highly placed former executives fill the roles of the new entrepreneurs. Among members of the New Jersey Association of Women Business Owners, and according to recent survey reports, we find a mixture of both former executives and former non-supervisory clerical workers. One survey of one thousand New Jersey small business owners, conducted by the Bank of New York in 1995, found that over fifty-four percent worked at a blue collar or non-executive white collar job prior to becoming a business owner.[2] Only one percent reported that they had been laid off, and only eight percent reported that they had been employed as executives. More than twenty-five percent of women owners in 1987 had ten to nineteen years of prior work experience. This indicates a long period of familiarity with business.[3] As Table 5 summarizes, among the women I interviewed, a large proportion possessed prior executive and supervisory work experience. From the national survey, we can see that sole proprietorship is not an elite activity. The study findings are atypical in the predominance of women with managerial and executive work experiences.

How did the prior work experience of white collar, middle-class women support their emergence as independent owners? When thinking about this process, it is important to consider that work is an ongoing process of gaining knowledge and interacting with others in business settings. Instead of a fixed set of skills tied to a job description that is plugged into an organizational structure in a prescribed way, skills are a variable collection of adaptable experiences that can be utilized in a range of business settings outside the one in which they are learned. The entrepreneurial strategy is an attempt by women in suburban New Jersey to control

TABLE 5. PRIOR WORK EXPERIENCE, U.S. & STUDY

TYPES OF PRIOR WORK	87' U.S. (N=6 mil.)	STUDY (N=35)
MANAGERIAL/EXECUTIVE	13.4%	43% (15)
WHITE COLLAR/SUPERVISOR	11%	09% (3)
WHITE COLLAR/NON-SUPER	23%	26% (9)
BLUE COLLAR SUPERVISOR	06%	02% (1)
BLUE COLLAR/NON-SUPER	16%	08% (3)
OTHER (STUDENT, HW)	11.4%	11% (4)
NOT REPORTED	06%	0
NOT APPLICABLE	13%	0%

U.S. Department of Commerce, 1992. N of companies with paid employees=1,656,575; women's share was 426,681. N of employees=62,951,041; women's share=6,965,037.

their work lives. Four women interviewed for this study describe their experience in the firms where they learned to do business:

I had ten years experience as a buyer in the garment center in New York City. I started with X&Y Personnel in 1971. I was a manager there, and I just decided if I could run somebody else's business, I could run my own business. And so I decided to go out on my own......I just figured I was going to do it for myself. But its a lot harder doing it for yourself, I have to say that.

The reason that was a fantastic job is because XYZ owned their own stores, so we had a lot of responsibility. I was responsible for figures, the bottom line, the programs, the performance of the stores and gross margin. I pretty much had complete say.

When you are working in a small business you can see how much sales you bring in and what the owner's profits are because of the work you are generating. ...I was able to increase sales and really make the bottom line for the company look a lot better. You realize that you can go on and do that for yourself. Then your efforts and your work and the time you put in will be rewards as well.

I was not able to go to college at that point in time, so I decided to get a full-time job to really learn about business itself.... At the same time I was able to grow and move up in the Bell system which gave me a lot of my background. Starting out as clerk-typist, the department started growing and started enhancing new types of equipment and me, always wanting to learn, I was always able to really end up in a position that I would test out or go beyond a pilot case... I opened up a new department. So that continued throughout my career with the Bell system. Right before leaving, which was a couple years after the break up (of the Bell System into regional companies), things started really changing. My last position there was manager for the administration department.

These women attained positions with decision-making responsibility. They do not report feeling alienated or limited by engaging in work, because cooperation within the constraints of their work roles gave them experience and forms of knowledge which they could use successfully in their businesses.

Corporations may constrain the opportunities of women, but these organizations also provide knowledge and experience about negotiation, management, and creation of value in the market. Even for those women who encounter particular managers who limit their careers, other opportunities for interaction give them confidence and alternative mirrors for their aspiration. They have been socialized to accept problem solving as part of their work roles. Corporate employment can involve creating a managerial self, as this woman owner describes:

> I went to work for Xerox. I worked for Xerox for about five years, and that was kind of challenging. That's where I discovered my talents for the business world, which I didn't know existed.

The business woman's recognition of efficacy reinforces a positive self-assessment, and her courage for independent action increases.

Individual bosses and supervisors can also encourage employees to form the discipline and interests that they later adapt to their careers as entrepreneurs.

> I had great mentors....[among others] he was always pushing me to be better. I couldn't be just a secretary for him. I had to be better than that.....And he was always pushing me to be better and be better and be better. You're in charge. You have to take down this information and you have to prepare these reports for me.

While women needed the training they received from former employers' businesses, they did not consider their increased skills to belong to the organization in which they were learned. Skills are interpreted as a form of compensation and social credit earned through hard work. As their contributions to the work process increased, so did their ambition and desire for control over the business. In the following quote an exporter reports how she tested the market and found clients:

I was working as an export manager for another trading company....I really wasn't happy doing that. I started to write a few of my old customers.... I explained to them that I was thinking of doing this on the side, and I would just handle their accounts. I got letters back encouraging me to do so. I think what really gave me that push is, within a 2 week time period, I was receiving checks from my clients overseas. And I hadn't even been incorporated, and it was just like, they really wanted me to secure the business for them. They were willing to pay in advance, to help me get started.

As employees who were given a wide range of independent action, women developed confidence for taking risks. They tested the waters, trying to determine what their work was worth and how much return they could receive from clients. Women weighed the promotions and opportunities open to them in salaried employment; they actively assessed their satisfaction and values in the process of making a decision.

The complexity of work and the independence available to individuals in the work place have been strongly tied to job satisfaction (Kohn and Schooler, 1983; Kohn and Slomczynski, 1990; Jencks et al., 1979; Spenner, 1983).[4] Kohn's work with Slomczynski (1990) and Schooler (1983) has shown that self-direction is directly related to the substantive complexity of work, whether in employment, school, or the home. Kohn and Slomczynski write:

the central component of self direction is neither freedom from close supervision, nor non-routinized conditions, but the substantive complexity of the activity. Engaging in substantive complexity one learns to value self-direction, enhances one's intellectual flexibility, and develops a self-directed orientation to self and society.... the experience of self-direction (in housework, schooling, other) not just occupational self-direction is what is important.[5]

Individual choices and strategies have a direct impact on the outcome of doing business, and the profits and rewards are not hidden by corporate supervision. Once liberated from the domination of bureaucratic work settings in which their business skills have formed, women can create new identities and offer new strategies for the organization of their lives (Goffee and Scase, 1985).[6] Three women report their enjoyment of making money, decisions and creative solutions to business problems:

...making money is very exciting except that we've been through such hard times these days, that's kind of been tough for a while. I think making your own decisions. Ah, just seeing the growth is very exciting; it's almost like your child. It starts up from the ground, and you see it growing into something meaningful. I still kind of get a thrill when people say, "Oh yeah, I know who Az Personnel is." Because it wasn't a franchise or anything. I just started Az Personnel from the ground up, and it's very nice to know that people know your company and who you are.

...when I was in corporate America I would put together these really in-depth programs and because of the political situation and who didn't like who, and which division didn't like that one, it literally would go on the back burner for a year and a half. So that was really quite frustrating because you couldn't do what you needed to do, your hands were tied. Here you try something, it works, it doesn't work, you get feedback, you try something else, so the ability to create something is very different.... Your identity gets all wrapped up in what you're doing. ....if an employee does something that you feel is not the way you want the company to be represented it really kills you. Inside its like, oh, how could you do that. It's hard to disassociate yourself from the business because you are the business. And in corporate America, even if you run a department, which I did, its not your company.

...Having the freedom to make choices.... I think that is what's most satis-fying. And for me, again its very satisfying because its always a learning experience for me.

A strong individualism pervades the testimonies of these women. They believe that every individual possesses the capacity to become who he or she wants to be. They believe that ordinary workers do not want control over decision making; they want people to make decisions and provide secure environments for them. In contrast to this stereotype of the employee, busi-ness owners have an ideal for themselves as people who take responsibility. They cannot depend on others to define how they should do business.

I'm very independent that way. I like making my own decisions, and I'm able to make those decisions without dwelling on the regrettable part of it. Right or wrong decisions, 50/50, and when you make it, you've made it, and I think that's one of my better qualities as an entrepreneur is that I make decisions. If they're good, I'm delighted; if they're not, I go on to the next situation, and I don't dwell on negatives. I'm very positive.

The individual's achievement of entrepreneurial independence creates high satisfaction with work in-itself, insofar as the individual identifies her life and her commitments with the value she produces. The entrepreneurial women I interviewed identify self-employment with control over their own work lives, control over the terms and conditions of work, its quality, and their own security.

LEARNING THROUGH NEGATIVE EXPERIENCE

Learning experiences can involve negative and positive interactions in the work place environment. Women, like other executives and workers, resent the demands of an employer for relocations and new assignments. The often contradictory tension between the individual's needs for recognition, a sense of efficacy, concrete rewards, and lack of control over their office environment emerge as an important experience for women who leave employment. Women entrepreneurs report that they do not like working in places where they are not given direct recognition and profit for what they do, despite achieving responsibility and finding complexity in their work. The two women I quote below could no longer accept the uncertainty of corporate control over their lives, despite their success:

> ...I knew I would never be given that kind of challenge again....And when I came back from Los Angeles, my job was gone. I still had a desk and a phone and a title, but the job itself was gone. And they wanted me to move....I had just reached a point in my life where I didn't want someone else making those decisions for me anymore.

> I was Vice-President of merchandising. The reason I left there was all the traveling overseas; my last trip was over Christmas; it was in Rumania. ...It was pretty bad. I decided I wanted a job in New Jersey.

The sources of dissatisfaction with salaried employment among women who became owners were social rather than material, and included the following factors: (1) The belief that the limitations of their roles in the work place were unfair, or being trained for management positions that were still subject to a pecking order internal to the corporation. (2) Employers did not give them credit for their talent and contributions; other executives and bosses took profit or credit for their work. (3) They lacked control over the rules and politics of the work place; they were asked to do business in a way they did not like. Four quotes from women entrepreneurs recalling their past work experience illustrate negative lessons:

> The major influence was the small business that I worked for down the hall.... he [the owner] was a horrible business person. He just did everything wrong. In my opinion he just did not service his customers. He didn't handle the orders well. He was totally disorganized. He tried to sell too much, too hard; every little thing that he could think of he tried to sell it. And you really can't do that. You need to focus on one certain product or a few that you know you can get to make profit from. And he wasn't

doing that. And I just saw him do so many mistakes I kept thinking to myself, I can do better than this.

Actually I made much more money as an independent rep. But the owners of the company had put in a new computer system and based their claims that this computer system had certain limitations (in calculating expenses); they were starting to play games with how they were paying our commissions. We eventually would get all the money, but it seemed like we started to finance our own jobs, our own production, which is what we needed them for.

....I think their egos just got in the way, they started to really play some games, and we weren't going to put up with it.

I would come home, and I would complain—this wasn't right. And the politics in an office, politics in anything drives me crazy. That's a problem that I've got is I call it "politics." You can call it human relations, but it really becomes politics.

In developing this department for them, after three or four long years, it was running itself, and I was not really moving. I was not doing anything at that point, and my goal was to really move ahead. ...probably would not have much of an opportunity to move ahead, at least within the couple of years that I saw.

I found a general cynicism about the legitimacy of authority in earlier encounters with corporate managers. Lower level managers and sales workers do not have executive control, despite the complexity of their jobs. They learn the business, but from a subordinate position. The women I have quoted feel justified in their criticism of their prior employers. I never heard anyone criticize herself for failing to adjust to workplace conditions. Their resistance to the conditions of earlier employment settings and their ambition to do things their own way were defended as rational responses to unfair limitations.

In hierarchies that may have internal pecking orders and informal networks with few women, creativity, hard work, and performance of complex work do not automatically lead to improved opportunities for managerial control. The following account by an exporter expresses the frustration of working in a corporate organization where her potential was limited by corporate structure:

So it was a big department with thirty people in my area. You know how departments are. You really can't do your full potential because it will upset everybody else that's in your area. So there is standard work that goes on. So anyone who really wants to achieve or really learn something

are really kind of held down in big business. That was my impression at
the time.

Working with others can involve limiting compromises that frustrate
motivated individuals. Although all human relationships involve some
form of control, entrepreneurs want to do things differently, their own way.

PERSONAL MANAGEMENT: A HEALTHY RESPONSE
TO UNCERTAINTY

Many women report that control over their business is a central value in
the organization of their lives. They want to stay in business on their own
terms. But control can be an illusion in small business ownership. Business
ownership, particularly in the first five years, entails more time than
salaried employment, great uncertainty, and an intensification of labor
under the constraints of contracts and demands of competition. What
women owners mean by control is freedom from direct personal subordination to a work regime that they did not create, not freedom from the
market economy or the rhythms of work itself. Two women I quote below
took control of the value and organization of their own time:

> you make your decisions, all the responsibility lays on you, and you don't
> have to abide by someone else's rules; you make your own rules.... there
> are certain stresses that you have when you're in business, but I felt more
> stress having someone tell me what to do and working fourteen hours a
> day, then me working fourteen hours a day and taking responsibility for
> making my own decisions and having free time when I want it and just
> running the show.... Everything that I worked for went to the business that
> was me so it was worth it. Not for someone else, you know you work
> fourteen hours a day and they barely appreciate it.....they just kind of
> expect that.

> I like being able to control my environment and what's going on around
> me. So I do like to know what's going on. And also I love the freedom of
> doing what I want to do when I want to do it. I really like to be able to
> do what I want. I've always been a night person. But I've evolved into not
> coming in until 11 o'clock and working until as late as I have to. Because
> I perform much better at night and I like the nights better. So, for me, if I
> had a 9-5 job I'm not sure what I would do.

The emphasis on control may also be a response to the uncertainties of
their past and present relationships in business or in their personal lives.
There are many possible sources of uncertainty, but common experiences
in contemporary women's lives include unemployment or downsizing,
divorce, a tight job market and career aging, as illustrated by the four New

Jersey business women who I quote below:

> ..I didn't have a vision of 'I want to own a business'. It was something that evolved because in looking for a job I was getting very frustrated and it sort of fell into my lap when I quit the job, and they said, "You want to take it free-lance?" and then it went from there. I went to a NJAWBO meeting; the first meeting I went to, I went home with a client. I had an appointment to see someone and signed up another real estate agent. And then I went to another meeting and I went home with another client. And then the art gallery that I was doing some work for had a major show, and I did the marketing for the show. And, as I said, I had been doing this stuff for a lot of years before I went out on my own. So it sort of happened.

> Divorce, which definitely made me realize I had to take control of my own finances and my own future and secure that not just for myself, but for my children. That was the major factor, I wanted to have control. Even when you are working for other people there really is no secure job out there. So I feel more secure knowing I have control over what I'm doing within my own business, than to be depending on others....

> When I left Bell, I was also going through a divorce. My family didn't really back me up, and I felt very alone, I suppose, so that I decided to leave New York. And I didn't want to go too far because I knew I would still want to be in touch because that family thing. ...So I moved to New Jersey and felt very isolated until I started networking and finding friends, individuals, who were really able to help me through a period of time in my life that was very difficult. Starting the business was a method of doing that because I knew at the same time I'd be able to make a living for myself, you know, earn some money to maintain my lifestyle of what I like to do.

> I graduated in 1990 and after graduation I went away for awhile and when I came back there were no jobs, because it was right at the beginning of the recession and I started working for a printer and that's where I learned to do everything that I do now. It was just a really bad job market and it (self-employment) was the best alternative.

The women I interviewed have different reasons for choosing to go into business for themselves, but at the heart of each woman's story is her attempt to control the conditions of her work life. Valuing control is a response to uncertainty and the desire to organize work in a fulfilling way. The owner who survives has to have discipline to start a business, practice the restraint necessary to stay with it over grueling work periods, and to reinvest what is necessary. She must want to control her own work process, to the point that she can resist the security of a steady pay check, or accept a lower income from the small enterprise. Conditions of uncertainty such as divorce, downsizing and career issues give women extra incentives for entrepreneurial risk taking.

CONTROL SHIFTS TO THE MARKET

Women trade one kind of control for another when they go into their own businesses. When an employee becomes an owner, important changes occur in the relationship to the production process. "Control" over work and the competitive costs of operation shifts from the relationship between management and the individual as an employee, with a salary and a budget for their department or function, to the diversified relationship between the market, clients for goods and services, and the individual as the owner of a business, usually a contractor, service provider or retail store owner. Control shifts to the demands generated by markets. The result is an intensification of the labor process for small firm owners trying to establish a secure presence among many other small firms in their niche.

This means compromise for entrepreneurs. A secure income is defined as a timely, guaranteed amount of pay. Replacing this, individuals must struggle to keep their clients and customers, find new business, and limit their costs, as this woman describes:

> It wasn't that I had long hours because there was that much work coming in. I had to really go out and see how much I needed, so it was more or less, gosh, I would say a good 8 to 10 hours a day just making phone calls, going out visiting, networking, and the whole bit. So I would say more like 10 to 12 hours really, I would say was being put in then. Now that business has picked up, and we're generating work to be done, the hours are longer. The hours have increased, but at the same time, I have been able to not diminish the market any but really kind of even it out. So I know there's a certain period of time I need to market my business in order to continue to grow, maintain it, and at the same time I've been able to bring on independent consultants who assist with the overflow that I can't handle, so in that sense, the hours are longer with the extension of the staff.

If business owners lose customers, or they cannot find new ones, their income will shrink, and so will their opportunity for self-employment. If profits from the business fail to increase, small owners will be unable to make insurance and retirement account payments. Owners drive themselves to work long hours, often in discontinuous schedules, in order to fulfill contract obligations. A discontinuous schedule means that time is put into the work when it is available, rather than time being measured in predictable blocks. One woman describes this:

> I guess at first I probably put in about probably 50-60 hours a week. And now it really depends if we're really busy, there was one week about a year and a half ago, I did 98.5 hours 'cause we were so busy I didn't have a choice, I mean I worked until 3 or 4 in the morning and then got back up again to get back here.

Small business owners may not have a reliable income, so they work when business orders come in. Women who own successful firms may choose to reduce their personal work hours, but this depends on the individual's attitudes toward the business and its managerial demands.

INDIVIDUAL DREAMS AND SOCIAL REORGANIZATION

People do not talk about a glass ceiling for working class people because it is assumed that they are permanently limited. The promise of liberation through participation in the market as a business person is held up as an ideal, and perhaps the only real way to gain control over the terms of identity. This proposition does not deny that there are structural conditions which bound or limit individual and collective experience. The interpretation of experience is a selective process which bolsters action through the individual's reflection on the sum of her experiences and her projection of what is possible. Two women describe their earlier working lives, when ideas and dreams were psychological motivations for 'just doing' things:

> My dream was always to be known, that people would know who I was, to make my mark. Until I was probably well into my twenties I never had any idea of what that was going to be. At one point, I thought it was going to be president of AT&T. You know that some day you're going to do something important, but you just don't know what it is. I never really honestly thought about having my own business cause I really didn't have that kind of a role model.

> Mostly a dream and a wish and an interest to do certain things and doing them, basically. Just not to be afraid to do things.....In the beginning it's very difficult. But as you do them over and over again it's easier. The blows are not as hard. You think you judge better than before. It's not as difficult as in the beginning. But you still have to try it.

By positioning their identities in positive references to success and dreams of creative efficacy, women subvert the assumption that they are socially and economically limited. As individuals interpret the possibilities for acting within the social and economic structures that shape their individual histories, they sometimes find the opportunity to expand their limits.

During the course of this study I met women whose businesses failed, or who recognized that the scope of their business was limited and less than they had hoped for. This office services and space provider uses popular self-help literature as a reference to position her current identity as a competent business person:

> I'd like to get into something that's creative, a little more creative, Because I have an artistic bent. So I'd like to do some desk top publishing....but as they say, 'when you're up to your ass in alligators, you don't have time to drain the swamp.'

After experiencing corporate downsizing, this woman received a small settlement, and she possessed organizational skills. Her status as a former manager for AT&T does not match her current position as an office services purveyor, with $40,000 in savings and a second mortgage tied to the success or failure of her small firm. The competitive niche of lower-end business services provides enough challenges to divert her attention away from any expression of self-denigration or defeat. In another example, a woman who produced several episodes of a canceled, ethnically-based cable television program for children still seeks funding for more shows. By putting "the whole package together," a series of coloring books and stories, she uses her artistic background to maintain her sense of efficacy, dignity and claim to the identity of woman entrepreneur.

Women who open firms have usually acquired the resources and the experience to pursue independent business through employment in corporations and other firms. The desire for autonomy from the managerial control of others combines with the ambition to be directly rewarded for individual talent and labor. The relative success women have experienced in lower level management and clerical positions has given them a strong sense of efficacy. Women in white collar support positions have learned the processes and values of market exchange, even though they may have only observed and aided the executive activities of others. White collar workers have organizational skills which are adaptable to independent business ownership.

Women business owners in New Jersey have turned away from positions of subordination in their earlier careers. Many of them believe that working for others involves too much compromise, frustration and uncertainty. There were some common sources of frustration with earlier employment experiences, which revolved around these women's perceptions of limitations in their roles as employees and their lack of control over work processes.

The theoretical assumption that women business owners were forced out of white collar and managerial employment in restructuring processes, and turned to small business ownership, was not supported by my study. A more complex and culturally embedded experience emerges from the women's narratives in which household and workplace organization lead individual women to assess their opportunities for control over their own work, and thus to pursue independent business.

CHAPTER NOTES

1. Howard Aldrich, Pat Reese, Paola Dubini, "Women On the Verge of a Breakthrough: Networking Among Women Entrepreneurs in the United States and Italy," *Entrepreneurship and Regional Development* 1(1989), pp. 339-356; Karyn Loscocco and Joyce Robinson *et al*, "Gender and Small Business Success," *Social Forces* 70 (1) (September 1991), pp. 65-85.

2. The Bank of New York, 2nd Annual Report on the State of Small Business in New Jersey, October 1995, p.6. Survey results are based on telephone interviews with the first 1,000 out of 8,000 owners who described themselves as a small business.

3. U.S. Department of Commerce, *Characteristics of Business Owners: 1987 Economic Censuses* (Washington, D.C.: U.S. Government Printing Office, April, 1992), Table 3, p. 12.

4. Melvin Kohn and Carmi Schooler, eds. *Work and Personality: An Inquiry Into the Impact of Social Stratification* (Norwood, NJ: Ablex Publishing Co., 1983); Melvin Kohn and Kazmierz Slomczynski, *Social Structure and Self-Direction* (Cambridge: Harvard University Press, 1990).

5. Melvin Kohn and Kazmierz Slomczynski, *Social Structure and Self-Direction* (Cambridge: Harvard University Press, 1990), p. 260.

6. Robert Goffee and Richard Scase, *Women In Charge* (Boston: Allen & Unwin, 1985).

The New Jersey Association of Women Business Owners

The definition of femininity held by the middle classes in the United States, and globally, has been undergoing changes in which women active in the public domains of business and politics assert new boundaries for "feminine" status behavior, and form identities as business women that have class symbolism independent from their attachment to the men in their families. A wider range of public action in market exchanges indicates higher social status. Women actively reinterpret the boundaries of their gender roles in business culture and attempt to transform that culture by continuing to participate in voluntary and business associations, as well as in business trade itself.

The New Jersey Association of Women Business Owners, a state affiliate of the National Association of Women Business Owners, serves as a site for the investigation of how associations shape individual identities and connect their members to collective agendas. The business association as a reference group for personal identity, and as a source of reference individuals or role models, establishes an affinity between the individual's experience in her environment, her self-concept, and the larger societal framework of meanings built around entrepreneurship. Smaller, informal relationships form through interaction in the association; these become the basis for temporary and spontaneous interactions which affirm and shelter individual identities within the normative boundaries established by the larger collectivity. Association helps each member to adjust to who she is, while maintaining the image of the woman entrepreneur as a successful cultural role to be valued and pursued.

Someone who wants to become an entrepreneur begins to imagine what entrepreneurs are like, how one should act and respond. The individual refers the self to other individuals and groups identified as entrepreneurs to help her develop an appropriate self-concept and social role. The businesswoman develops a personal investment in the definitions and norms she interprets when she interacts with entrepreneurs or group members who function as reference individuals. These reference individuals act as role models for individual performance, and as people who affirm her identity as one who belongs among them.

Many small business owners aspire to belong to the reference group of wealthy entrepreneurs who represent success. The leaders within the New Jersey Association of Women Business Owners represent diverse paths to entrepreneurship. The association exhibits a high degree of tolerance for differences in age, wealth, and social capital among its members. The association gave me access to its influentials, well spoken, established individuals to whom I could refer, deepening my understanding of the association and the emergence of the woman entrepreneur in suburbia. I was fortunate to interview two state presidents, two local chapter presidents, two chapter officers and a former local chapter president. Their encouragement and endorsement softened the way for my approach to other members of the association. These activists were embedded in other business networks in their state and region, especially the Chambers of Commerce. Profiles of six popular leaders in different chapters highlight both changes in the history of women's roles in business and the acceptance of diversity in chapter leadership. Barbara, Ellen, Donna, Shannon, Tina and Andrea are fictitious names, but their stories are biographical and factual.

ELLEN, BY HER BOOT STRAPS

In 1992, at the age of thirty-three, Ellen was the President of a large, central New Jersey chapter. She owned a corporation specializing in staff recruitment, in which she worked up to seventy hours per week. After six years, she employed eighteen workers. Although Ellen dropped out of the local state university, her business experience is extensive, having started in her late teens. Ellen attributed her life long desire to own her own business to the stresses of helping her immigrant mother negotiate a divorce from her father. Ellen became convinced that her mother received an inadequate child support and alimony settlement, and she swore to become an attorney or someone with enough money to protect herself. At the time of our interview, the support and security of her family were paramount concerns. Ellen's two young sons, one seventeen months old and another five years old, were cared for by a full time nanny. Ellen's husband worked in her corporation as a Vice President, and they enjoyed a supportive relationship. A Republican and a self-identified conservative, she worked hard to influence and educate the political views of chapter members. Under her leadership, her chapter hosted local politicians as speakers.

DONNA, A FAMILY BUSINESS MBA

Donna was thirty-two years old in 1992, newly married for one year to a young Christian minister, and childless. Donna's office was located in the former den of her suburban home. This was her second attempt at establishing her own firm; her first business failed. At the beginning of her entrepreneurship in 1989, she worked eighty to ninety hours a week, whenever she wasn't sleeping. In 1992 she worked fifty-five hours a week, and managed two employees. The daughter of a family in the same industry, Donna was socialized to assume a leading role in her family's small business, designing marketing programs, plans and research projects in regional service markets. She was raised with the expectation that she would take over the firm. Her father trained as an artist, but he became an entrepreneur to support his household, while her mother worked as a secretary. Donna worked for other businesses large and small in similar industries before turning to entrepreneurship. Donna earned an MBA from the state university, and was educated about economics and business organization. She believed that her last employer was unethical because he worked for competing clients and lied about it. Donna was also very uncomfortable when a clique in the organization forced the firing of the only black employee after manipulating and scape goating him in an internal office dispute. She held a low opinion of her former employer, but regarded most people in her industry as worthy of her respect. A regional representative within NJAW-BO, Donna was thoroughly professional, knowledgeable, and comfortable with herself. She was active in her church, voluntary and industry associations, including the Chambers of Commerce.

TINA, THE SELF-MARKETER

Fifty-one year old Tina survived the downturn of 1989 to 1992 by shedding her three employees and moving from a professional building on the highway back into a small office in her home. In 1992, after eleven years in the advertising and marketing business, she employed one part time worker and one worker on a project basis. One of her employees was a struggling entrepreneur who worked for Tina while she tried to raise capital for her own projects. Tina worked seventy to eighty hours per week for her business. A former school teacher, Tina served as an officer in her local NJAWBO chapter. She opened her business during a period of unemployment, after resigning from a local corporation because of dissatisfaction with management. Tina was happily married to a corporate manager, whose income provided support while she struggled to build her client base. Her two children were adults, thirty and twenty-seven years old, who no longer resided with the family. Tina admits that it was hard for her to work while they were children because of the expectations of her family that she should be a full time mother. Her parents were conservative Jews.

They expected Tina to devote herself to being a full time housewife. She is proud of achieving an independent career. Tina is highly respected and adept at marketing her personality and identity through business associations. She frequently refers to her life history as a common touchstone for women's lives.

SHANNON, SUPPORTING HER LIFESTYLE AND HER CHILD

At the age of forty-five, Shannon was the leader of a small, southern chapter of NJAWBO. She rose through the ranks to achieve state office within the association. As both salesperson and service provider in her business, she traveled throughout the state, working up to sixty-five hours per week. As a suburban housewife with a part time job, she had experienced a painful divorce and became the sole support of her only child. Shannon became self-employed after a long period of trying to establish a career. The impetus for becoming self-employed was a sexual harassment experience with a former boss. At the time of our interview, Shannon's twenty-two year old daughter was a college student who resided out of state, and also belonged to NJAW-BO as an associate member. Shannon is a lesbian, but she does not reveal her sexual orientation to clients. The other members of her chapter are aware of her sexual orientation, and there is at least one other "out of the closet" member of her chapter. In 1992 Shannon's one employee was a young welfare mother trying to work off the books while she searched for a way to support herself and her child. Their relationship was friendly, and Shannon interpreted her employer role as helping a good person to survive. Shannon was a self-described liberal, a feminist, and a lifelong member of the Democratic party. She holds a Bachelor's Degree from a college in the City University of New York. Her desire to have a government which is supportive to both women's rights and gay rights motivated her to participate in the National Organization for Women, as well as local service associations. Shannon served as State President of NJAWBO, and today she continues to be a prominent organizer.

ANDREA, BEYOND CORPORATE MANAGEMENT

Andrea was a corporate manager with a major telecommunications corporation prior to opening a business. In 1992 she was forty years old, divorced and childless, but sharing a suburban house with her female business partner. Her business was seven years old, and employed one full time and four part time employees. She dates men when she has time. Andrea grew up in a lower middle class southern family. Her father worked as a specialty cook and her mother was a housewife. She went into business for herself because she was tired of corporate reassignments and having no control over employer demands. During her corporate employment, Andrea was always planning for her future by taking courses. Andrea achieved an MBA from a local private university. She participates in several voluntary associations, marketing herself through organization networks. Andrea is an issue-based Republican, socially liberal but fiscally conservative. She served as a state president of NJAWBO and sat on the board of directors of the National Association of Women Business Owners.

BARBARA, THE NEW GRADUATE

In 1992 Barbara was single and twenty-seven years old. A graduate of an elite, private college, she was the president of a large northern chapter. Barbara is one of a new generation of women in business who have never known the absolute barriers to women's leadership that were common less than twenty years ago. She was childless, although she wanted to marry and raise at least two children. Barbara went into business for herself through her affiliation with the northern chapter of NJAWBO. She began attending meetings while she was still employed by another small business owner, who left her in charge of processing orders while he traveled. At first, in anticipation of marrying and having children, she wanted to own a home-based business. As she learned more about business through NJAWBO, other business owners became clients and credit references. Her goals changed; she focused on building a list of clients. Barbara continued to work in a local firm while she established her business. Her father was a small business owner, and her mother was a teacher. Barbara continued to live with her parents, who lent her the money to open her own business by taking a second mortgage on the family home. She put in fifty to sixty hours a week in her service firm. Barbara reported that she was always a well organized, analytical person, but business ownership required her to become more diplomatic and less defensive with other people. Barbara worked closely with one full time employee of the firm, a woman in her twenties who she treated like a partner. Her family members are Democrats, and Barbara spoke at length about protecting a woman's right to choose an abortion as a motivating political issue. Nonetheless, she was a strong proponent of traditional gender roles within the family, and she aspired to give up business and volunteer full time after marriage. Barbara eventually went out of business in 1996, and took a position as a salesperson with a large telecommunications corporation in another part of the country.

The suburbs are not the uniform social landscape that we might assume when confronted with popular images of the nuclear family ideal (Stacey, 1990). Six women, including three mothers, one married with young children, one divorced with a grown daughter, and one married with grown children, along with three childless women, one single, one married and one divorced, were able to achieve leadership positions in their local NJAWBO chapters. The chapters rewarded the voluntary participation of these women, regardless of social status issues such as family, household

Table 6. THREE ASSOCIATION LEADERS, STATE OR REGIONAL LEVEL			
Characteristics	Shannon	Andrea	Donna
Position	President	President	Regional VP
Business	Insurance	Investments	Marketing
Age in 1992	45	40	32
Marital Status	Divorced	Divorced	Married
Children	1 (Over 21)	None	None
Employees	1	5	2
Years in Business	12.50	7.00	2.50
Personal Income	$30,000.00	Not Reported	Not Reported
Business Gross	$62,000.00	Not Reported	Not Reported
Hours	65 per week	60 per week	60 per week
Highest Education	B.S. Phys. Ed.	M.B.A./C.P.A.	M.S. Marketing

Table 7. THREE ASSOCIATION CHAPTER OFFICERS			
Characteristics	Barbara	Ellen	Tina
Position	President	President	PR Chair
Business	Typesetting Design	Human Resources	Public Relations
Age in 1992	27	33	51
Marital Status	Single	Married	Married
Children	None	2 (5 yrs, 17 mo.)	2 (Over 21)
Employees	1	18	2
Years in Business	5	6	11
Personal Income	Not Reported	$80,000.00	$49,000.00
Business Gross	$162,197.00	$850,000.00	$300,000.00
Hours	60 per week	70 per week	70 per week
Highest Education	B.A. Psychology	H.S.	B.A. Education

structure, or level and prestige of education. The members of the New Jersey Association of Women Business Owners represent a middle class civic culture that seeks to reward individual initiative rather than strict conformity to corporate or patriarchal ideals.

GROWING NUMBERS AND CULTURAL CHANGE

As the number of independent business owners grew after 1970, the membership and activity of business associations increased. Of thirty small business associations listed in the *Encyclopedia of Associations* (1995), twenty were founded in the fifteen-year period from 1975 to 1990, sixteen of these between 1980 and 1989. The United States Chambers of Commerce, founded in 1912, grew from 36,000 members in 1967 to 80,000 in 1974. Membership more than doubled again between 1974 and 1980 (Vogel,

1989).[1] The U.S. Chambers listed 219,200 members in 1995. The membership of the National Federation of Independent Business, founded in 1943, grew from 300,000 to 607,000 between 1970 and 1995.

These associations may be seen as one variety of "voluntary association," organizations formed to further the common interests of members independent of government. Membership in these associations is neither mandatory nor ascribed; it must be actively chosen by individuals. "Voluntary associations" are nonprofit organizations with aims designed to benefit the whole society (Sills, 1968). Political parties, churches and business associations fit the broad definition of voluntary association, but they are usually studied separately from other nonprofit organizations, maintaining a distinction between benevolent behavior, and self-seeking or self-interested economic and political behavior.

Voluntary associations mediate the culture of civil society and politics in the United States, establishing connections between their membership, the general public and the government (Lipset, Trow and Coleman, 1956; Sills, 1968; Tilly, 1981; Tocqueville (1835) 1990; Wolfe, 1989).[2] The representation of the group's interests to the public is part of its attempt to shape culture and social organization at the local level, as well as to influence the distribution of resources to the needs of its constituent members. Thus, these grass roots organizations are important to the analysis of social change (Sills, 1968; Tilly, 1981; Weber, Vol.1 1978; Wolfe, 1989).

Voluntary service organizations have frequently acted as a socially conservative force by upholding the patriarchal family and male leadership as models for civic and business participation. Women's roles are at the center of contemporary changes in voluntary associations traditionally associated with small business owners. Both the Elks and the Buffaloes refuse to gender integrate their leadership, relegating women to auxiliary clubs composed of the wives and female relatives of male members. As late as 1995, 2,236 Elks Lodges with 1.3 million members in the United States, were still debating whether or not to remove the word "male" from the association's constitution.[3] Women can become members of the Elks's women's auxiliary if they are first nominated by a member, and are voted in by the club. The Lions Club, another voluntary association with a membership that includes many local business owners, maintains a separate woman's club division, The Lionesses. Lionesses are given recognition as separate but equal leaders of association activities. This sex separatist strategy on the part of these groups led one of the speakers at an New Jersey Association of Women Business Owners meeting to characterize the Elks as "dinosaurs."[4]

The male fraternal culture of these organizations is threatened by the emergence of women business leaders. This threat is more pronounced when women business owners are not attached to males as family members. Until 1989, membership under the Rotary Club Constitution was for men only. Changes in the sex-typed membership rules began in 1978, when the Rotary

Club in Duarte, California invited two women to become members, causing the Rotary International to withdraw the club's charter.[5] A lawsuit against the International was upheld in Duarte's favor by the California Court of Appeals (1986), and the United States Supreme Court (1989). Many conservative local clubs still maintain separate women's sections, called Women of Rotary, Rotary Ann Clubs, Las Damas de Rotary, Rotary Wives or The Inner Wheel. The separate women's groups in Rotary pursue service projects that reflect traditional "feminine" concerns such as baby clinics, day care centers, schools, food and clothing drives, homes and services for the elderly.

During the 1970's, barriers to women's participation fell in the Chambers of Commerce, making way for a new generation of leaders. By the 1990's women emerged as prominent regular members in both the Chambers of Commerce and Rotary Clubs in urban and suburban areas. In 1995 a woman was hired to serve as State President of the New Jersey Chambers of Commerce. Voluntary service and business associations in New Jersey, New York and California have led the way toward a gender integrated future for women in business and civic leadership. Women have become activists for local business interests which were once represented by men only. Despite these advances, women must negotiate their acceptance in associations as individuals, while beliefs about traditional roles continue to influence how both men and women assess impressions about business aptitude.

Social historians have documented ways in which segregating women and men into separate gender activities has supported social stratification based on male lines of inheritance of property. In patriarchal history, women held status insofar as they were related to men as wives, relatives or mistresses (Coontz and Henderson, 1986).[6] Women's segregation into separate spheres of activity restricted their independent access to resources. Males in the dominant status group exercised the power to include female members of their class, and recognize women as equals, or to restrict women's participation and ignore their independent action. Despite advantages, women remain subordinate within dominant classes. Such segregation forces women to conform to normative, sexually controlled, types of behavior if they wish to be included or recognized. In studies of Medieval industry, Martha Howell (1986) discussed the ways in which peasant women enjoyed a wider range of behavior than women of the gentry and upper classes. Peasant women shared work with men in the fields and around the cottage, but upper class women had to adhere to more restrictive segregation of male and female activities in order to preserve the norms of femininity which identified them with elite status (Gilchrist, 1994).[7] Both men and women have to interpret the boundaries of gender roles in business culture, but higher status activities in business reinforce dominant masculine styles. As women gain access to managerial positions in business, they shed their reticence to transgress subordinate feminine roles.

THE NEW JERSEY ASSOCIATION OF WOMEN BUSINESS OWNERS

In response to the rising number of independently owned businesses during the 1970's, The New Jersey Association of Women Business Owners (NJAWBO) was incorporated in 1978 through a creative alliance between local business owners and a state government committed to the integration of women into business at all levels. The United States federal government has always recognized business and trade associations. Small businesses distribute goods and services, provide employment, as well as produce local leaders and organizers for political, charitable and economic activities at the community level. Small business owners have a direct impact on the organizational strength of civil society. The symbolism of alliance between government and small business owners is achieved by funding education and self help programs that are advertised and partially funded by the United States Small Business Administration. The symbolic alliance can also become a concrete basis for political action and mobilization, for example in the passage of The Small Business Act of 1997, or in the solicitation of the voluntary sector by Vice President Albert Gore to support the Welfare to Work Initiative.

In 1992 one of the original founders of NJAWBO, Bette Benedict, a small business liaison with the New Jersey Department of Commerce, was among a small group of active association members who maintained an alliance with the state and federal governments. Governments must guarantee individual rights and market integration. If they wish to improve the collective position of women in the economy and society, it is important for women's organizations to be connected to government liaisons, officials and legislators. Women struggling to increase their share of the market in competitive industries keep a sharp eye on the development of government regulations and policies that have an impact on business owners. Betty Benedict maintained the state government's connection to a local base of organizational support and sought to strengthen the goal of women's full integration and equal participation. In part, this was her job as a functionary of the state bureaucracy, but she maintained a strong sense of the history of women in business and the importance of collective organization.

Betty Benedict was a career woman in New York City before she and her husband moved to New Jersey. As suburbanites in the 1960's, they lived through the early feminist movement and saw the economic emergence of women in the paid economy. Benedict built a career as a public relations executive in private industry before joining the state government of New Jersey. Part of Benedict's job with the Department of Commerce included working with the Small Business Development Centers. Adele Kaplan, another NJAWBO founder, was the chairperson of the Centers, which were partially funded by the state of New Jersey to provide advice and education for people starting businesses.[8] Adele Kaplan helped adapt the bylaws of New York City women's business clubs to the New Jersey organization's charter and rules. There were many women involved in planning the organization, but at its inception, an agent of the state and a local activist adapted existing organizational forms to establish a women's business association. The campaign to organize an association that would capture at least part of the diverse waves of women entering business ownership began with an exhibit for the New Jersey Association of Women's Business Owners at The Women Business Owners Educational Conference in 1978. The "Women's Expo," was held at "the Club" in Giants Stadium in the Meadowlands section of New Jersey. According to Benedict, no women had been in the Club for a women's event before. This created an exciting feeling that women could break old barriers by collectively organizing to support one another.

The corporate structure of NJAWBO was formulated to be similar to other club and service organizations, such as the N.J. Chambers of Commerce. Local county chapters elect officers, and send representatives to regional and then state committees which develop the strategies of the organization. Service on the committees is voluntary, and the length of service at the state level usually determines who will be state president of the organization. Only active members hold office.

An "Active Member" of NJAWBO is a woman who is a sole proprietor, a partner owning at least fifteen percent of the partnership or corporate shares, or less than fifteen percent if the corporation is fifty-one percent women-owned, and she holds a policy making role; or a woman who financially maintains business facilities as her major source of employment and income (including commissioned agents, brokers, independent contractors, and consultants).[9] The central tenet of the definition is executive control or management by a woman owner. Associate members who cannot hold offices include students, government officials and family members.

NJAWBO included fifteen chapters in 1992, and membership was estimated at one thousand members, with a monthly active membership count of 856 in June of that year.[10] It is not a large association by American standards. In 1995 this was one sixth of the membership of its parent, The National Association of Women Business Owners, founded in 1974. The current structure of NAWBO, the national organization, includes forty state organizations. In comparison, the National Association of Female Executives (NAFE, f. 1972), had more than 250,000 members in 1995. The American Business and Professional Women's Association (ABPWA f. 1949), had 90,000 members including assistants, secretaries and executives who do not own a controlling interest. But NJAWBO is for women who own and manage businesses.

The owners of independent businesses actively network at the community level of society and the state level of government, creating a dynamic local base for political and social activity. Even if the majority of small business owners, like the majority of Americans, are not 'joiners' or regular participants in these organizations, voluntary associations represent the interests of the group to the public through media and outreach events, and to the state at all levels by lobbying candidates, elected officials, and participation in policy formation through research publications. Local association chapters and clubs articulate shared values and ideals for the business community as a whole. Often, small business owners disagree about how to define common issues and concerns. It is difficult to achieve a universal vision of the collective good at the local level. Individuals disagree about what their relationship to the state should be. Associations provide forums in which business owners can discover shared concerns, discuss common ground and connect issues to local politics.

Charity events also bring the skills and resources of local business owners into the spotlight. A national survey of women business owners found that seventy-eight percent volunteer, compared to fifty-six percent of all business owners.[11] Women hold strong ties to their local communities, and they recognize and reward volunteer commitments. Small business groups organize, fund and contribute to the full spectrum of volunteer community events and organizations, displaying their organizational talent outside their businesses. The redistribution of modest wealth and knowledge through these strategies builds public good will between peers and other members of the polity. The events also allow people to include spouses and children, adding a personal side to their public personas. Spouses of executives gain social status by participating in club activities that have community functions.

NJAWBO sponsors the EXCEL Program, an education and mentoring program for people who want to start businesses. EXCEL provides new entrepreneurs with an assessment of their aptitudes, and a short, intensive course on business skills. New business owners are brought into the association and adopted by older members. This facilitation of business formation and education is subsidized by the U. S. Small Business Administration and the New Jersey Department of Community Affairs. But even without the grant monies they receive, the teaching and mentoring programs are a popular way for women to participate in NJAWBO. Self-help can be extended to helping others.

The association aims to tie members to both national and international networks of information and potential connection. The connections are more symbolic than real for the majority of the membership. NJAWBO is an affiliate of the National Association of Women Business Owners (NAWBO), incorporated on December 19, 1974, by women who sought to exchange information and develop business skills. NAWBO is affiliated with Les Femmes Chefs d' Enterprises Mondiales (World Association of Women Entrepreneurs), which in 1992 was associated with organizations of women business owners in twenty-three countries, organizing 33,000 members across the globe.

Although only one woman in this study does business internationally, the idea that there are thousands of women across the globe actively organizing businesses is exciting to others. Several women mentioned the national and international scope of the organization's network. The promise of national and international connections has the symbolic function of locating the individual in part of a larger global world economy. By imagining they are part of a universal exchange in which women are important leaders, members of NAWBO and NJAWBO overcome the patriarchal prejudices that women must remain tied to local and household economies. The global scale and scope of NAWBO promises that commerce will lead to a more successful future for women.

NATIONAL ASSOCIATION STRATEGIES

Among its many activities, the National Association of Women Business Owners, the parent of forty state affiliates such as the New Jersey Association of Women Business Owners, functions as a marketing group for women entrepreneurs, corporate products and services, and the political lobbying agendas of association members. The National Foundation for Women Business Owners, NAWBO's non-profit development and training foundation, combines the primary research and education functions of the association with marketing products and an image of the woman entrepreneur designed to attract powerful sponsors. The mediation of information and image is the part of the mission of NFWBO, whose statement reads: "The mission of NFWBO is to support the growth of women business owners and their organizations through gathering and sharing knowledge." Knowledge is a selective process of organizing data both observed and interpreted, combined with verifiable statements or analyses and theories about what is claimed or known. The language of marketing becomes an activist strategy in the struggle to improve women's status in business and establish opportunities for better market positions.

NFWBO "research reports" present a dramatic selection of statistics and claims, establishing an equal or sometimes superior role for women in the economy and polity, as this quote reveals:

> Women-owned businesses are growing by leaps and bounds ...making them an increasingly attractive market for many corporations. The nation's nearly eight million women-owned enterprises employ one out of every four company workers and contribute $2.3 trillion to the economy, according to NFWBO.

> For nearly a decade, major corporations have benefitted from NFWBO's research findings to make key marketing decisions. NFWBO has demonstrated that women and men entrepreneurs have different thinking and

management styles that can impact the ways in which they research and acquire products and services.[12]

Women entrepreneurs' choices are idealized to parlay the impression of success, a strategy which should attract capital resources and corporate sponsorship. The claim that women behave differently from men in their purchasing decisions maintains corporate and public interest in appealing to women owners as a separate group among the self-employed. This "information" strategy also legitimates the existence of NAWBO as a separate gender-based association devoted to correcting misimpressions about women entrepreneurs. Women's social status rises with their access to people in power and the institutions which support elite cultural roles. In a report titled "2020 Vision: Entrepreneurial Policies for the 21st Century," the National Association of Women Business Owners presented the recommendations of two corporate sponsored think tanks in March 1995. The foreword to the report proudly claims both corporate ties and gender progress:[13]

> Sponsored by IBM, these meetings took place at the Cosmos Club in Washington, D.C. The club itself is a symbol of changing times: the former all male bastion, its walls coated with photographs of Nobel, Pulitzer and other prize winning members, just elected its first woman president.

The image of women breaking the barriers to gender equality in corporate sponsorship, private clubs and powerful prizes, legitimates the power of those institutions. Such images also align the interests of women entrepreneurs, the majority of self-employed women who employ no one, with both leading women entrepreneurs and conservative, wealthy corporate forces in the society. Despite the small scale and modest contribution of the majority of self-employed women, association with elite individuals increases the social legitimacy of all women entrepreneurs and eases the way for greater public acceptance of women in business.

None of the women I met in New Jersey own businesses that are large in scale, if this is defined as having a significant share of production or service in a national market. Nonetheless, many small business owners aspire to grow firms large enough to hold national prominence. The association is a launching pad for ambition rather than an elite club. The courage and vision of most women business owners is not small, local, or only focussed on lifestyle and family interests. The aspiration to be a bigger player in the business world survives.

CHAPTER NOTES

1. David Vogel, *Fluctuating Fortunes: The Political Power of Business in America* (New York: Basic Books, 1989).

2. Lipset, Seymour Martin, Martin Trow and James Coleman, *Union Democracy* (New York: The Free Press/Anchor Books, 1956). David Sills, "Voluntary Association," In David L. Sills, ed. *International Encyclopedia of the Social Sciences* 16 (1968): 357-379. Louise A. Tilly and Charles Tilly, (eds.) *Class Conflict and Collective Action* (Beverly Hills, CA: Sage Publications, 1981). Alexis de Tocqueville, *Democracy in America, Volume One*, [1835, 1945] (New York: Vintage Books, 1990). Alan Wolfe, *Whose Keeper: Social Science and Moral Obligation* (Berkeley, CA: University of California Press, 1989).

3. *Los Altos Town Crier*, "Palo Alto Elks Lodge No. 1471 says Ono' to Accept Women," [1995] http://www.losaltosonline.com/latc/arch /9538/TC12a_-_elks.html [July 21, 1998].

4. Union County Dinner Meeting, Featured Speaker, November 10, 1992.

5. Women in Rotary, http://www.rotary.org/press/index/ women_ri.htm#Background [July 28, 1989].

6. Stephanie Coontz and Peta Henderson, *Women's Work, Men's Property: The Origins of Gender and Class* (London: Verso, 1986), pp. 108-55.

7. Roberta Gilchrist, *Gender and Material Culture: The Archeology of Religious Women* (New York: Routledge, 1994); Martha C. Howell, *Women, Production and Patriarchy in Late Medieval Cities* (Chicago: University of Chicago Press, 1986), p. 10.

8. Interview with Betty Benedict, New Jersey Department of Commerce, Small Business Liaison, Trenton, New Jersey, July 28, 1992.

9. New Jersey Association of Women Business Owners, *Fact Sheet and Application*, Bridgewater, NJ, 1992.

10. New Jersey Association of Women Business Owners, "1992 Membership List," Internal Document.

11. National Foundation for Women Business Owners, *NFWBO News/ 1st Quarter 1997*, Silver Springs, MD, p. 3.

12 National Foundation For Women Business Owners, *NFWBO News*, 1998 (1): 1 & 3.

13. National Association of Women Business Owners, "2020 Vision: Entrepreneurial Policies for the 21st Century," (July 11, 1995), p. 2.

Marketing Selves Through Association

Associations offer support to both individual and collective small business owners. They provide forums in which a member's identity and reputation can be built while she acquires information and organizational skills. With the everyday pressures and stresses of performing as a small business owner, an individual may find it desirable to associate with others in business, to share and establish a stronger identity for herself and for the public image of the firm. Some of the cues which affirm that an individual holds a particular status or identity come from who they are surrounded by (Goffman, 1959).[1] Small business owners spend long hours with their employees, and with potential clients. It is a relief for them to interact with other small business owners who understand and affirm their middle class cultural status as well as business identities. NJAWBO gives members the opportunity to seek out more successful and established individuals and to form relationships with local leaders. With success dependent upon interpersonal processes, such as self-presentation, connections with others, and effective interaction, participating in business associations helps individual women to compete for opportunities in markets.

Individual adjustment to the entrepreneurial role causes changes in social interactions which support the self and social personality, as these four women recall:

> I think you become a little more positive, bossier. A lot bossier.... You have to be a jack-of-all-trades. You've got to keep encouraging. You've always got to be working very hard; you never can feel like, "Oh, this is a piece of cake." You always have to work very hard, put a lot of yourself into it, and try to get your employees to feel the same way...

> it definitely matured me faster than I would have if I had just a job. ...there's so many stresses and there's so much responsibility that you can't

help but grow up to be able handle them. I've learned to be much more diplomatic over the years.

I have to say that the growth process was incredible. One thing that amazed me was I became a much nicer, more relaxed person, and I think a lot of it had to do with being more in control of my own life. Being able to make my own choices. I became much more confident in dealing with people and with business issues because I didn't have to worry about people second-guessing me in terms of the decisions I was making.

I became much more self-critical. Whether you have a success or a failure, you immediately say, what did I do that was right? Or what did I do that was wrong? You think you need to project an image that isn't real in order to get yourself to the next phase; and sometimes you're way off.

Changes in identities may also be connected to the differences between "corporate" and shop based environments. According to this partner in a cleaning service, transitions between corporate and entrepreneurial identities were not easy to negotiate:

I feel that's who I am. I'm the person in the suit. That's part of my identity... Giving up the term "manager" in a big company was a little bit difficult, but then I became an entrepreneur. That was a different kind of identity, and it was like, "I own my own business." ...it was tough because it wasn't a professional kind of business [cleaning service]. So that was a really hard transition.

Corporations define work roles for women independent of the family, which support middle class or white collar identities. The "suit" once signified managerial or middle class status. The individual belonged to a group with authority derived from a place in the structure of a corporate hierarchy. As an independent small business owner, authority must be built through a wider range of relationships. The individual must signify that she still belongs to the managerial middle class, but without the assurance of power vested in the offices of a large organization. Without the support of a franchise or network selling organization which provides a package of marketing techniques and materials, the independent woman entrepreneur must market herself. The daily work of the entrepreneur involves continuously marketing the business, her efficacy as an owner, and her vision of the future, or what she expects to accomplish. This process can be challenging for individuals who have not been socialized to work in open market conditions.

The business person needs a group in which to learn the norms necessary to operate in local, regional and national markets. He or she must construct a distinct identity for the firm in relationship to competitors. The owner and the firm then achieve or occupy some status position within the market.[2] Business associations can introduce women to entrepreneurial, small business culture and provide them with opportunities for interaction. They integrate individuals into the local economy by strengthening their identities as owners and defining agendas for collective action. Belonging to an association is not a necessary condition for operating a business or succeeding in one, but it can serve as a useful resource.

Individuals who are new to business ownership or who are not part of established family businesses are strongly attracted to association claims. Regional entrepreneurial networks are sometimes dominated by established families that give leadership roles to relatives. For example, Marcy Sims of the Sims Clothing Store chain in New Jersey is a leader in the family business who appears frequently in the press and media. But for an individual starting a new firm without such familial references, there is a need for a group or collective forum in which identity can be established and affirmed. In the past, social support for the small owner may have been provided by family members or church or temple congregations. But in the contemporary suburbs, individuals may not have social ties to other people who have the time to be concerned about their business. Spouses work full time and focus their energies on their own workplaces and careers.

The entrepreneurial ties formed in a small business association go beyond the economic and include social support, legitimation, exchange of information and personal recognition (Freeman and Keels, 1992).[3] These intangible benefits can be blocked by other kinds of status apart from gender, such as race or cultural norms specific to urban or suburban settings. But social interactions are important to constructing an identity for the business in the market and an individual definition of self as an effective entrepreneur. A market 'self' cannot be created without the recognition of other people who support the individual's identity. One informant who was active in both a women's association and the Chambers explained how NJAWBO helped her to create an identity within her locality:

> I don't know about the actual revenues... They've helped me as a business woman. They've helped my image in the community. Because they see me, they know who I am and then they kind of know who Corp X is. So, I can't say that I can relate it to actual dollar amounts. But I would say that yes, it's helped me and my business and helped me grow. I pick people's brains when I meet them. I kind of find out how they do things and what they do and what's going on with their business. . .

The business focus of NJAWBO distinguishes it from other voluntary associations such as the Rotary Clubs, which perform community service. Another quotation illustrates NJAWBO's all-business agenda:

It was a ready and accepting network of people in positions similar to mine who were starting or in their own businesses, and who wanted to talk about business. Its not a sit around and talk about your grandchildren club; its for people who want to talk about business.

Association friendships offer sources for the practical understanding of everyday business problems and solutions to them. Researchers in business and network studies have shown that during the process of organizing and managing the business start-up, entrepreneurs learn how to answer questions, solve problems and provide encouragement (Smeltzer & Fann, 1988; Freeman and Keels, 1992).[4]

.... I am very active in the Chamber also, and there are people who are small business owners, and we share war stories and so on. You understand. It's the same mentality. Professional people, I don't care if it's a male or female, they don't know what it's like. I didn't know what it was like! I don't understand what's its like when you're laying awake saying, "Oh, God, this is coming due, and let's see, what's the aging report? When can I start calling for this?

And the market is turned and all of these contracts that we thought we were going to get, and maybe they aren't coming, or Gee things are terrific! They don't understand what it's like to have a business. I didn't. So again, I don't really care if you're male or female; it's a business owner, a person who understands what it's like to be there.

Values concerning types of action must also be consistent with collective norms. New business owners are sometimes uncertain or ambivalent about using certain practices. For example it may be "normal" to stall a business creditor in order to meet your payroll while waiting for account receivables to balance. As this entrepreneur explains:

I never pay cash for anything. When times are tough, never pay cash for anything. A little cash can be used for a lot of things. Never pay your bills early. If you've got thirty days, take thirty days. You can never guess how much cash you can get on the street, and you get it from your vendors.

Operation of a small business is demanding. New owners sometimes cannot adjust; they need education and advice.

Within large corporations there are institutionalized controls over projections of future action. Managers fail quickly in the corporate organization if they do not accomplish what they have proposed to do (Jackall, 1989). Corporations provide both institutional and informal social controls over behavior, demeanor and action. In comparison, the small business owner is less subject to controls of this sort. Customary norms of behavior are maintained through repeated interactions with other people buying, selling or trading goods and services, not necessarily on a daily basis. A small owner who wants to increase her client base frequently gives a low bid, to attract more business and keep current clients. But owners contracting with too many new clients are always at a disadvantage in bargaining over the value of their service or work, because the unequal distribution of power affects the terms and execution of the work contract. A small business owner who is late with projects may stay in business for a long time by continuously seeking new clients. But with a limited service, the new client or customer may choose not to continue doing business. Thus, for every new client, the entrepreneur must expend energy developing a relationship that is not yet established over the long term. The new business owner may make too many promises and end up in a terrible struggle to accomplish what she has promised, or to maintain more affluent appearances than she can afford. A member reports:

> There's a lot of people who come out of large business and they start little businesses, and they don't know what to do. They're used to having a staff; they're used to calling up someone and getting their supplies, so that doesn't happen in a little business, and it takes a lot of time for someone with that background to understand how a small business works, and a lot of them wash out.

Uncertainty about who you can trust with the resources in a business, and the limited sources for small start-up capital, lead small business owners to rely on friends and relatives as advisors. They depend on strong ties in their working lives (Birley, 1985; Aldrich, Rosen and Woodward, 1986).[5] But the resources, information and imaginations of this familiar group may be limited. The information available through networking in associations can open alternative sources of capital, ideas and knowledge, strengthening the individual's strategies for negotiating business. Granovetter (1973) proposed that "weak ties," or dispersed acquaintances, provide bridges and links to many networks that have a wide range of information and resources.[6] Business associations give frequent seminars on how to network, how to make connections, and how to raise capital. Whether the individual participates in an association or not, she must make an effort to interact on a regular basis with other people in her locality, market and industry. Associations offer tested strategies for pursuing social ties, so the individual does not have to imagine or discover ways of connecting to others. Collective knowledge about norms of social interaction then become valued legacies of group participation, not site specific to association meetings or limited to association members.

The New Jersey Association of Women Business Owners did connect some women entrepreneurs, but did so less than individual members expected. These two owners recognized that social acceptance built trust over time:

> It's taken a while for me to get business out of NJAWBO. I think if people go into NJAWBO thinking, "OK, I'm in business and I'm gonna get business." That's the wrong attitude. People need to trust you—I don't care who you are or what you are—people need to trust you as an individual before they're going to refer people to you, before they're going to give you their business.

> Its not like going to the supermarket and handing the lady five dollars and getting something. In an organization like that you have to contribute, and give it at least a year before you get anything. If people think you're just there to get something for yourself and not give anything, they're going to avoid you like the plague.

People talking favorably about a friend or associate in an organization create trust which is the basis for public reputation; these social judgements are in turn shared by members who are "regulars" in the local Chambers of Commerce and business circles in the state. Such connections augment the reputation a business builds through customer word of mouth recommendations. Local networking strategies may eventually connect local entrepreneurs to state and regional opportunities, despite the lengthy trust-building time taking place in association meetings. Individuals practice the networking strategies in their business or social lives learned within the association. Not all individuals are secure enough or have the necessary interaction skills to increase their range of alliances and friendships. They run the risk of appearing weak because they cannot sustain a wider public reputation based on extended social ties.

NJAWBO members always have someone to call when they need the answer to a problem, or just someone to talk to. For example, while I was sitting in a NJAWBO member's office, the telephone rang. "I'm being interviewed!" my informant told another NJAWBO member, briefly explaining who I was and what I was looking for. "Are you interested?" She scribbled her friend's name and address on a piece of paper and handed me my next connection. Members informally vouch for one another and make connections for friends and business owners recommended by other members. A member summarizes:

> Networking, the development of support systems in terms of having someone else that's done the kind of the same thing that can identify with the frustrations that other people around you can't identify with, the education in terms of providing a lot of educational opportunities, especially for new business owners.

My study supports others that have found that networking outside family relationships provides social support (Tausig and Michello, 1988),[7] legitimation for action, feelings of self-confidence and personal power (Smeltzer and Fann, 1989).[8] A "self-made" woman or man needs other entrepreneurs with whom to interact and to provide group identity. No individual can be motivated to become a "market actor" independent of a culture that values business.[9] In the words of a young designer:

> ...NJAWBO was amazing.... the women who were there in the beginning before I had my equipment - because I used to introduce myself and say I have a company called . . . but I don't have my equipment yet so I haven't started. And those people were just so supportive. Like you can do it, you can do it. They didn't even know me that well. But because they wanted to help, they support women business owners, they gave me so much support that I could not have done it [without them].

There is also the common experience of loneliness that comes with not being part of a 'work group.' Epstein (1989) and Garson (1975) both found that people enjoy participating in a culture of the workplace, sharing a common sense of identity with others in the same work roles.[10] But what happens when the owner is alone? The "sole" proprietor may be the only person in her office for most of the working day. Two members describe their need for support:

> I tended to look for affinity groups where I could find other women business owners which is why I'm now a Regional President of NJAWBO. I needed to find other people who were in similar situations because after I left my father's business I couldn't come in and just find someone to talk to. It wasn't that he wasn't interested, its that he just wasn't there day to day, and how many times can you call somebody and complain.

> [the association] kind of does away with the isolation part of being a business owner because you can establish your network, your core of individuals who share the same things. We're all independent—we have that in common, a lot in common.

Participation in the association relieved loneliness for some women. Social interaction relieves the uncertainties that can paralyze an individual manager's decision making process.

COPING WITH BARRIERS

A person's gender or race status may act as barriers to social recognition as an entrepreneur. If these social status markers create uncertainty, doubt or fear, the entrepreneurial "face" may be contested or broken by hostile pat-

terns of communication.[11] The individual's credibility and legitimacy may
be a silent issue in interaction. The cultural legacies of racial, ethnic and
gender exclusion influence the judgements of other people in the business.
A woman entrepreneur recalls how a black co-worker was eliminated from
the small corporation in which she was employed:

> When it would come review time they would put things on the review like,
> doesn't work well with outside suppliers. You know with all the equal
> opportunity things, there was a lot of emphasis on advancing minorities.
> They got him fired, and it wasn't that he was incompetent. They were in
> bed with the VP [covering up unethical business practices] and they
> manipulated the whole thing [scapegoating the minority] and got what
> they wanted out of him.

When women and minorities in business encounter racism and sexism,
these prejudices become part of a bargaining process in which the individual is forced to prove the legitimacy of her participation. She may be drawn
into more difficult bargaining terms, or positioned in ways that make it
harder to profit. Two women describe the sexist interpretations that they
sometimes encounter in their businesses:

> I definitely have situations where I'll be standing in the business with one
> of my employees. Somebody will come in and go right to him assuming he's
> in charge because he's a man. And he's not. Both men and women do that.

> Women have to continually prove themselves, I've found. Even at this
> stage with my business being successful and six years old. I do get treated
> sometimes as if, I was initially asked and I am still asked this today, "Well,
> what if you decide to get married and you want us to sign a contract with
> you; you might just go." Women are still looked on by some individuals
> like these are hobbies and pastimes. Until they find a man and settle them
> down; and that is very frustrating at times.

Business owners call the sale or order a "moment of truth" in which
the contracting party must be assured that the owner can fulfill his or her
commitments. This means assurance that the identity and representation of
the business are trustworthy. The moment of truth puts the credibility of
the person's identity as a business owner on the line. Race, class and gender biases in the culture can create doubts about legitimacy, and the suspect
individual may be ignored. NJAWBO teaches its participants to strengthen
presentations of self and to negotiate personal anger and resistance to
women in business, rather than engaging in frustration, retreat or protest.
A successful negotiator recalls benefitting from being a woman in male
dominated environments:

Most of the things I do are male dominated. There are people out there who don't know how to deal with people who are different from they are, and you just have to deal with them. I don't think there's any great conspiracy against women. I don't think we have to take on some crusade, because that turns people off.

In the same way, ethnic and religious business associations function to affirm individual and collective identities while strengthening the individual's ability to negotiate with other citizens outside their personal reference groups. Rather than a individual response to social exclusion based on shared status, such as class, race, ethnicity, religion or gender, joining a business association can reinforce collective identities that are not otherwise at the center of business. One effect of participating in a group of women is that the association can diminish feelings of exclusion attributed to gender minority status. Social codes and norms that influence trust precede exchange, and shared cultural status is one basis for individual trust and collective security. Emotional and personal feelings are also invested in a shared sense of belonging which reinforces investments of time in an association.

The struggle to manage perception about the prestige and size in the business was difficult for some of the women I interviewed. They confessed to me that their business was not as secure as they portrayed it. An owner seeks to control firm image as much as possible. Many small owners will not reveal their income or the amount of capital in their business, because they do not want to be perceived as too small. Small business owners understand that they must organize the perception about who they are and what they offer for business reasons. By creating doubts in the minds of potential clients, their reluctance to reveal their small operation can also create the impression of insecurity. They may thus defeat the attempt to sustain the appearance of success.

Small owners have good reasons to feel anxious about their size and reputation. Robert Merton coined the term the "Matthew Effect" to explain how rank is connected to recognition and rewards; scientists with higher status positions in academia receive greater recognition and rewards for accomplishments than do scientists who hold less prestigious positions (Merton, 1968).[12] Joel Podolny (1991), an economic sociologist, found that the Matthew effect operates in the investment banking industry. Those banks with higher rank have the advantage of lower production and advertising costs because they attract more business on the strength of their reputation; they also receive larger orders. They can offer business products and services at a lower cost than new firms competing for recognition. Lower status producers are forced not only to meet the standards of the leaders, but they must struggle to change how their businesses are perceived by other actors (Podolny, 1991). The perception that a business is of low status makes it a less desirable trading partner. By the same token, a high status producer cannot enter low status niches in industry without compromising or risking the perception of market position (Podolny, 1991). The relative market power of different size firms gives larger firms the added value of defining standards for production and cost efficiency.

Although reflected in reality, the public perception of women's firms as smaller, poorly capitalized newcomers in market competition lowers their perceived status and creates a barrier to trade. A small firm may thrive by producing in specialty niches which are too small to attract large producers. A prominent Middlesex County box factory owner competes with large producers by taking contracts for small "runs" or numbers of packages, and offering customized services. A small firm may also survive market competition by offering boutique or craft quality products which are alternative to mass-produced offerings, or customized services such as investments, handmade leather goods, customized mechanics, and gourmet foods.

Business associations open a dispersed range of opportunities to make connections, and the diversity of interactions gives the individual the freedom to construct an identity that reflects her values, confirms her personal stake in the legitimacy of her business, helps her to maintain a competitive base of local knowledge about practices and connections. The eventual success or failure of the individual business may depend on market demand in commercial "niches," but associations offer social strategies to establish identity, presence and a base of support in a locality or region.

CHAPTER NOTES

1. Erving Goffman, *The Presentation of Self in Everyday Life* (New York: Doubleday, 1959).

2. Joel Podolny, "The Matthew Effect and the Constraints of Status: A Sociological Perspective on Markets," Paper Delivered to the American Sociological Association, August 1991, p. 4.

3. Elizabeth Byrne Freeman and J. Kay Keels, "A Framework of Entrepreneurial Networking," Paper, American Academy of Management, August 1992.

4. L. R. Smeltzer and G. L. Fann, "Gender Differences in External Networks of Small Owner Managers," *Journal of Small Business Management* 27 (1989): 25-32.

5. Howard Aldrich, B. Rosen and W. Woodward, "Social Behavior and Entrepreneurial Networks," in *Frontiers of Entrepreneurial Research* 1 (1989): 239-240.

6. Mark Granovetter, *Getting A Job: A Study of Contacts and Careers* (Chicago: University of Chicago Press, 1973).

7. Michael Tausig and J. Michello, "Seeking Social Support," *Basic and Applied Social Psychology* 9 (1988): 1-12.

8. L. R. Smeltzer and G. L. Fann, "Gender Differences in External Networks of Small Owner Managers," *Journal of Small Business Management* 27 (1989): 32.

9. David McLellan elevated this need to the primary motivation for entrepreneurial achievement in *The Achieving Society* (New York: The Free Press, 1961).

10. Cynthia Fuchs Epstein, "Workplace Boundaries: Conceptions and Creations," *Social Research* 56, 3 (Autumn 1989), pp. 571-590. Barbara Garson, *All the Livelong Day: The Meaning and Demeaning of Routine Work* (New York: Doubleday, 1975).

11 The term "face" refers to the individual's ability to sustain an identity, to manage a consistent impression, during interaction with other people in a defined setting. Erving Goffman, *Presentation of Self in Everyday Life* (New York, Anchor Books, 1959).

12. Robert K. Merton, "The Matthew Effect in Science," *Science* 159 (1968): 56-63. The term refers to the Book of Matthew in the New Testament, "For unto everyone that hath shall be given, and he shall have abundance; but from him that hath not shall be taken away even what he hath (*St. Matthew*, 13: 12)."

CHAPTER SIX:
Meetings, Social Rituals of Interaction and Exchange

Meetings provide social rituals of exchange in which social definitions and boundaries are negotiated. Like members of other associations of business owners, the members of NJAWBO define the use of the term entrepreneur, create rituals for the presentation of self as an entrepreneur, and establish ideas about the "true" woman business owner. The association sustains a symbolic community, "women owners" or "women owners in this county." The established entrepreneurial role is favorably compared beside the part-time business owner, who buys and sells on the side for a little extra money. But individuals who attend meetings may not possess the criteria that compose the definition of an entrepreneur. The community comprises women who derive their primary income from a business they manage full time, women who plan to start a business, women who have lost businesses, students, retirees, male allies and part time contractors. By interacting within the association, individuals come to understand the association's ideological definitions of an open, socially democratic market and their positions relative to the group's values.[1]

CULTURAL SETTINGS AND PROCESSES

The typical setting for interaction in the New Jersey Association of Women Business Owners is a breakfast or dinner meeting in a small banquet room of a local restaurant or hotel. These spaces are designed for middle class business travelers, small conferences and local events. The meeting formats include (1) networking, or meeting and greeting people, (2) announcements, (3) introductions, a ritual presentation of self by each member, (4) ancillary speakers and expert guests (bankers, resource people), (5) main speakers with a program theme, and (6) a question and answer period. Over the course of two hours a number of identity building processes take place: personal recognition, the construction of a common culture, political socialization, practical education and information, and networking opportunities.

Formal and informal interactions between members and guests take place during meetings, in a time schedule related to the organization of an event. To establish or manage individual or group identity, contributions to the organization become a form of earmarked money, taking on a symbolic exchange function or culturally defined social meanings (Zelizer, 1994).[2] Dues money and meeting fees symbolically assert a social identity, "business owner and entrepreneur". Before the meeting begins several members volunteer to handle the door. One member collects the $22. fee for attendance or checks the prepaid participants off a list. Every participant wears a name tag. Individuals congregate in the back of the room before they move to a small group or find a place at a table. Small groups form throughout the room as members stop to talk to one another. Regular participants usually gravitate toward the leaders who are setting up the event. New members and occasional participants tend to stay in the circles in the back of the room unless they are invited to be part of the program.

This is an important time for informal interaction. New members are brought into conversations with one another and with established members. Individual goals are communicated to the group. One woman is looking for an employee. Someone has been offered a contract she cannot fulfill, and she offers to connect another member with the business contact. A first time participant is introduced to other members. They ask about her business and make suggestions about how she can pursue new contacts.

Even these casual patterns of interaction have cumulative effects on the individual's identity. Associations are made of many "interaction shelters." Interaction shelters are temporary and unplanned interactions of short duration, which involve quick but important acknowledgments of belonging. In spontaneous, selective interaction individuals who have common social interests and experiences can express alternative norms, share information, support strategies for building positively valued identities, and find ideas for strengthening the goals of individuals in the group. There are different "clearings", opportunities to interact spontaneously, in which collective meaning and individual identity emerge. People create their own social circles within organizations, even taking part of a meeting room for self-selective seating or conversation.

During my first meeting I was greeted by four women in a small group who asked about my business. I was accepted as an aspiring sociologist and potential future business owner by people who barely knew my name. After the group broke up, individuals mentioned me to friends while they made their way through the assembly. At another meeting I attended, I found myself in the company of three strangers who were new members of the association. I learned that two of the three women were not making a profit from their business. They were sharing their husbands' salaries and trying to build a client base. One was a product designer and the other was a bookkeeper. When I asked if they considered themselves home based workers, they objected to the term. The location of the business was not their focus of self-definition. Both women left full time employment in large corporations to subcontract for independent business. Yet they still defined themselves as managerial and creative individuals trying to capitalize on their skills. Their clients came from connections with their previous employers, and a current concern was how they could build a client base beyond their present connections. They struggled to find enough clients to support true independence from previous employers. The third woman was in full partnership with her husband in an auto body shop in Edison. She was a classic 'wife as business partner', but she assured me that the business was half hers. In my first introductions with this group it was clear that we were women who had worked continuously throughout our adult lives. As a temporary small group we reassured and engaged one another in supportive interaction concerning our individual identities and business goals. On other occasions I was accompanied by association officers who introduced me to members of the association.

My observation of these small groups in the informal networking times revealed the degree to which many participants did not meet the organization's definitions of entrepreneurs or active members. Many of these women were still dependent on male incomes, or they were partners in the same business with a spouse. They continued to depend on the material and emotional support of a husband while they tried to launch an independent business. Their career opportunities were limited, they confessed, so the choice of self employment offered an option out of working in dead end positions. Each woman defined herself as a business owner who valued her labor. They did not express the "I want to get rich fast" arrogance of television commercials for courses in real estate or franchise entrepreneurship. Their presence at the meeting indicated that they were committed to building a client base. The association reinforced the ideal of transcendence of wage employment through market participation and independent ownership. Women were encouraged to define themselves as owners even if only aspirants.

Public places where conversation and interaction occur on a regular basis also can support an individual's identity as a business owner. Favorite bars, cafes and restaurants are still common daily sites of familiar interaction. But the association meetings create opportunities for interaction in public where individual recognition of the owner status is guaranteed among both friends and strangers. The introductions in NJAWBO meetings highlight the social and affiliation functions of association, as distinct from purely instrumental, informational purposes.

CLASS AND STATUS

Despite the egalitarian interaction patterns of the small, informal groups in the association, class and status distinctions did emerge among members. Business success and size are automatic bases for status in the association, but voluntary service also creates ties of friendship and solidarity. Active members who have achieved high status know one another well; they serve on committees together, and look out for one another's interests. They are an inner network of people committed to the organization. The insiders were clearly dominant at the open meetings. But the presidents of the chapters and members of state offices changed in elections held once a year. Presidents were not allowed to serve more than one term. Everyone in the organization knew who the individuals in line for leadership positions in the next election would be, because their candidacy was based on their length of service to the organization. They worked their way up the association's committee system of leadership.

The owners of modest businesses increase their status with frequent participation in NJAWBO meetings, events, and committee work. Any woman can build her status and reputation in the group by volunteering to work with the Association's committees. The leadership works to reward her commitment by word of mouth references. As one said:

> Every time you work with an organization like NJAWBO and you participate, everything you do comes back to you..... Every one of those jobs (four offices) has taken a lot of time and a lot of energy, and every one of them I've walked away saying, "I've gotten more than I've given," whether that's in business, in knowing more people, in contacts, visibility, whatever those are—feeling good about something you've accomplished....

Individuals can develop new skills and connections through service participation while they also increase their importance to the association.

> NJAWBO has provided a very good forum for me to grow as an individual. One of the things that I have accomplished as a member of the board is to extend myself, to try things that would have been a little bit scary for me in the past. And I've grown as an individual through my roles in the organization which is why when I tell people about networking, I tell them get on a committee. Get involved in something where you can get the support of other people to accomplish something because those skills you can take with you in your business.

Unlike the market, the inner circles of regular participants could be entered without increasing their monetary investment. The voluntary system of participation mirrors the democratic ideal of the market itself as an open venue for social mobility. There are alternative systems of prestige, including business success and the social recognition built through volunteering. These alternative sources of social status create "defacto authority" in the organization.[3]

The President of the Middlesex County Chapter in 1992 exemplified the association's democratic market ideals and the reality of its status patterns. An attractive blond woman, thirty-three years old, and about five feet four inches tall, she owned a human resources (employee leasing) corporation with a payroll of twenty people. Her youth distinguished her from women owners who were in their forties or fifties, with years of work experience behind them. She had worked full time since she was nineteen years old. She was the mother of two sons under the age of six. Her chapter thought of her as a leader with admirable courage who faced the challenges of parenthood, marriage, business management, and political leadership. Her personal history exemplified the ideal of the democratic openness of the market, but her business success represented the power of status derived from success.

In the small group around the Chapter President was a member who was also well respected in the association for creating wealth with a box factory and real estate investments. She provided work for her family, including her husband, a former jazz musician, and other family members. Her daughter's printing press had been financed by her mother. A representative of a local bank stood beside her; he was working to promote a new loan program for small business owners. The banker wore an expensive, conservative dark blue suit with a white shirt and modest gold jewelry. Although women wore different styles of outfit, everyone could clearly be identified as suburban middle class. Clothing from middle class and discount department stores, such as Macy's, Sims and J. C. Penny, far outnumbered costumes from Saks Fifth Avenue. All wore attire that symbolized democratic conformity to the norms of market participation. But among the members of NJAWBO seeking first loans and advice about business growth, signaling self-indulgent consumption on too grand a scale could damage their chances of gaining help. "Power" suits signify the ability to participate in society at higher levels of status, but clothing that is too costly or formal can also intimidate others, creating a barrier to a shared sense of belonging. "Power" has to appear legitimate, earned through hard work or intelligent investment of resources. Every business person becomes a sociological observer, reading the diverse signifying patterns that make people feel comfortable interacting within and between social class categories.

Performing with egalitarian demeanor during the informal networking times in the organization was an important part of the social code for participation in the association on a regular basis. The self-made woman cannot afford to exclude herself from potential business connections; symbolically she will not raise herself above the conversations, introductions and negotiations which simulate the social processes of the 'open' market. During NJAWBO meetings, creating the impression of friendly intimacy with other members, even in the absence of trust, reinforces the idea that the market will free the individual from other effects of social prejudice. In this way association meetings differ from interactions in first meetings between business people and sales calls involving people who do not know one another.

There were very few minority women, either of African or Asian descent, at the NJAWBO meetings that I observed. Their participation was pointed out to me by members of the chapter leadership, who expressed a commitment to multi-ethnic equality. This was hard to achieve with so few minority members. Their participation legitimated the ideal of an open social exchange process, but it was a challenge for the association to attract enough members from non-Caucasian backgrounds to exemplify the ideal. Members were not obligated or forced to interact within the association. Individuals frequently sought other women with whom they shared social characteristics, including common ethnic, racial and religious identifications. The conformity in dress, deportment and ideology that the association exhibited gave individuals the opportunity to interact without acknowledging social divisions. Association participants are in the contradictory position of claiming that anyone can achieve entrepreneurial success, while they aspire to greater social status above others. Members thus affiliate with prejudices about social identity which position the participant in existing relations of class, race and gender. Business ownership is embedded in systems of class and group status maintained through social relationships, but the interactions that sustain those relationships involve pretending that social status boundaries are open negotiations of both value and identity.

INTRODUCTION RITUALS

Every NJAWBO meeting opens with a round of introductions after the presentation of the meeting agenda by the chapter president. Going around every table clockwise, each woman stands in turn and introduces herself. A supportive round of applause is offered for each woman's accomplishments. There is approval for the aspiration to appear in the world and pitch oneself. Each "face" is accepted uncritically in the main forum of the meeting, while individuals are privately evaluated by insiders. This acceptance communicates symbolic equality and belonging.

The women's association is open to people who aspire to business ownership. It is not easy to immediately evaluate a person's claims about herself or her business status during the introductions. Business ownership as a claim to a potentially higher social status can act as a disguise in social interaction. The claim to ownership may be a device for increasing the apparent status of the individual, making her more interesting to established business owners, bankers and other service representatives who attend meetings as guests. The disguise temporarily allows someone to participate as an equal in the association, when they are not qualified to do so. This mask can hide unemployment, bankruptcy, small partnership, the most tenuous start-up, and failure. Members cover for one another, providing ongoing encouragement for the individual who is struggling to achieve. By forming insider status groups of women known to own thriving businesses, association members pursue their own interests while continuing to provide help to new owners.

RECIPROCITY

Among the women in NJAWBO I found that established owners enjoy mentoring women who are just starting, or planning to start a business. The information, knowledge, experience and social support they share with new members reinforce and clarify their own practices and sense of legitimacy. Legitimation through communicative interaction is reflexive and mutually reinforcing for both the experienced owner and the initiate, but it has the greatest impact on the self definition of the new owner. Business owners find that it is gratifying to see that others have experienced similar problems and fears, and that they appreciate the advice and counsel of people with practical experience.

The commitment of successful members to the education and support of new members and even women who aspire to own a business is a primary function of the organization. One woman describes this experience:

> Sometimes you don't give yourself the credit you deserve. But if you can see yourself reflected back from other successful people—you got to remember, these are very successful people—and if you can see how they perceive you, especially that it's in a positive light, that really helps you feel good about who you are. And for me that was one of the best things that happened in NJAWBO.

The simple recognition of a person as a business owner combined with the social reinforcement of her goals and choices are important ways in which identity is reinforced in the organization. Each chapter hosts an awards ceremony to recognize its contributors, leaders and new members.

There is a stratification of local businesses, and relationships of exchange and friendship develop through self-selective networks. A reciprocal exchange of services is a common way to share in one another's success. A business owner can find other members who provide insurance, investment planning, employee training manuals and contracts, advertising, newsletters and other services.

Independent professionals are the traditional, stable backbone of middle class small business in American society. A professional degree is unlikely to fail for a competent dentist, doctor or lawyer. People with Masters Degrees and Ph.D.s have also joined the ranks of independent business owners, often specializing in different kinds of life style and organizational management.[4] Through voluntary business associations, independent professionals and entrepreneurs in business reinforce a local alliance between independent professionals, traders in goods and services, and local banks.

Women's associations cannot replace the general market around which individual industries are structured, but women tell each other that they are using a NJAWBO business. NJAWBO provides a structure of references based on the trust built through interaction in the association. When an owner receives an opportunity from another association member, it asserts the bonds of trust that are formed during regular participation. As one noted:

> But what's happening now as people get to know me, I'm getting referrals now from my other business too. And it's like anything else, you lay the groundwork and it builds up slowly, but then it starts coming faster and faster. Like E. just called me this morning about this person from Union County. Why? She knows me. She trusts me. She knows who I am.

These reciprocities remind members of the value of association which affirms one's own identity and choices.

The opportunity to build a new self is one reason for women to join the association. NJAWBO meetings were in part a stage show of confidence, through which members could build a stronger sense of purpose through the positive reinforcement of accepting each other's claims to status and identity. As we see in this quote:

> I'm always dressed for work in case someone comes in or I have to appear. And there's an aura of that "I'm successful," even if I'm not. The worst of times, you have to put on a facade. You can cry on somebody's shoulder, but to the public you smile. And you can say, "Things are lousy, but they're getting better." And that's another thing you can do at NJAWBO. You can say, "Business could be better." And "Business is great," and we share good news and bad news.... part of my thrust was to become involved. And as soon as I became involved.... I did the whole marketing bit, and it all worked.

The meeting is a space in which a new self can be constructed through interaction. When an individual appeared to be open to interaction, she increased the likelihood of attracting and influencing people who shared her interests.

KEEPING UP APPEARANCES, FEMININITY AND CLASS STATUS

Maintaining the perception of femininity was a concern for some members. A chapter in Northern New Jersey in 1993 held a meeting with the theme "Maintaining Femininity in a Masculine World." The anxiety that the feminine was diminished by interacting continuously with men in male-typed activities weighed more heavily on some women than on others. There was sufficient anxiety about crossing cultural gender boundaries to sustain several meetings on image management over a five year period (1990-1995). Such meetings continue to be a regular feature of the chapter schedule.

Cultural boundary maintenance is fundamental to conformity in the performance of work place norms (Epstein, 1989,1992).[5] How can a woman conform to the norms of gender and business roles? The association reassures participants that there is no contradiction. The leaders believe that conformity to the rules of capitalism will provide opportunities for individuals regardless of their sex, although the normative performance of gender must be observed. The identity of "women owners" reiterates a binary opposition as "minority" in relation to the dominant male "mainstream" which many association members are uncomfortable with. But femininity as an individual gender performance is valued as a necessary conformity to societal and market codes of behavior.

Class status is also interpreted through the presentation of a gendered self. One of the greatest barriers I found while conducting my field research was a reluctance on the part of my informants to discuss their failures and set-backs with an outsider, or someone who might judge them deficient in their actions and decisions. Individuals try to keep up "successful" appearances, reinforcing the impression that a well dressed, feminine woman carries high social status. People dress "up" for meetings to signify success and personal confidence.

Even within the circles of association, women often had only one or two very close friends with whom they would share the full range of their fears and problems. For example, a mother with two small sons referred me to her best friend, also a mother with two small sons. Neither woman worked at home, and they relied on full time sitters. Illnesses, emotional issues, time constraints, and a whole range of social issues were important topics in their shared friendship. Mutual aid in the form of social and emotional support helped both women to overcome the guilt and anxiety caused by being away from their children. Emotional reciprocity was an important resource.

THE PROGRAM

After the rounds of introduction, the regular program features presentations by experts and service professionals. For example at a large Middlesex County meeting in 1993, two representatives from NatWest Bank, one woman and one man, emphasized the availability of small business services and loans, from those offered by the small branch manager in New Brunswick to the medium size business loans from a manager with an office in Edison. The bankers wanted to make a good impression; they seemed genuinely eager for new clients.

In part this was the bankers' public relations performance. These institutions offer a wide range of services for the small business market, including payroll accounts, mortgages and investments. Even in predominantly white middle class suburbs, banks are often criticized for not making enough small business loans. Low capitalization makes small business unattractive to banks, regardless of the ethnicity or gender of the business owners. Many small business owners purchase second mortgages for their home or vacation property as a way to raise capital. By making a friendly show of support for NJAWBO, the bank attracted a range of different business. The lure of the business loan could turn into the reality of the second mortgage or the "convenience" of checking and payroll accounts. In the 1990's small business loan funds and strategic loan marketing by banks became more common because retail credit studies showed that profitability outweighed risk for loans to women. The bank offered an open door to the small business, and this provided legitimation to its institutional role and market interests.

In my interviews all the business owners referred to the value of self-education that was offered through the association programs. The chapter programs always included practical education in business topics. A regular participant recalled the positive experience of the organization's programs:

> A couple of the most important activities are getting involved with different kinds of programs that can range from enlightening the group on insurance opportunities, government and state opportunities, ways to cope with stress, how to deal with managing your business, so the variety of the programs that are available is tremendous, are good.

Consultants and inspirational speakers establish themselves in local circles of association. Other business owners make presentations about financial planning, adapting to changes in the market, and employee leasing plans. The women I interviewed expressed a strong desire to be recognized for the quality of their service. As one woman put it, 'I don't need something outside, a big title; the power doesn't interest me. I just want to be recognized for what I do.' The solicitations of service professionals in these meetings flatter the participants with recognition for their role in creating the market.

The program presentations include prescriptive advice to people who are considering starting a business. I witnessed frequent themes during meetings which I synopsize in the following statements: "Forget the dream of ownership if you do not have a clear idea of where you are going or how to finance it." "A business plan is the only way to get a loan." "Adapt to changes in the market or become a dinosaur waiting for extinction." "Don't gamble with your retirement account." "Employee leasing can save you money." "Form of incorporation and tax structure are related."

During the networking periods that followed the formal meetings, individuals were free to seek help, connections, references, and simply to talk to their friends. Business owners sought reliable answers about how to collect unpaid invoices, how to keep track of what they were investing in the business, and how to negotiate with difficult clients. This kind of information is available from established business owners who know the folkways and norms of negotiation in an industry. For example, it is not unusual for established business people to use credit or a late payment as a temporary loan, but new business owners may panic when their invoices are past due because they do not know how to press for their interests with clients and vendors. To a new owner, a seasoned owner's experience can make the difference between adequate cash flow and continuing relationships with clients and suppliers, or broken relationships and bad credit. This kind of knowledge must be gained by interacting with other people in an industry.

The association exhibited a moderate amount of goal displacement among smaller chapters. Goal displacement is the tendency of the group's leaders to focus on procedures and rituals of order as ends in themselves, rather than as a means to the stated goals of the association (Merton 1968, Sills, 1968). One year a new chapter president in a small, regional chapter chose to abolish the rounds of introduction before the program. Regular attendance dropped and the chapter regulars had difficulty attracting new members. The ritual of introductions was reinstated with quiet expressions of relief by members that 'finally everything was back to normal'. Small chapters focussed on ritual order and social activities such as boat cruises and basket raffles. Large chapters like Middlesex and Union counties had developed political and social agendas for making their group influential in the community and the greater polity.

Individuals are not liberated from economic and social divisions, but the groups in the association shift the focus of interactions from race, class and gender, to individual status evaluations among women who regularly participate. Status is measured in ways that provide opportunities for business women to attain recognition, by business size and income, as well as by individual volunteer service to the association. This allows women who may not be able to achieve a public leadership role through the financial success of their business to attain recognition and affirmative social goals by participating in a women's association. The ambiguities attached to female gender roles and the range of action open to women are allayed by norms controlled by the consensus of the group.

CHAPTER NOTES

1. While I was not able to observe deal making, I was a participant observer in five meetings of the New Jersey Association of Women Business Owners during 1991-1993.

2. Viviana A. Zelizer, *The Social Meaning of Money* (New York: Basic Books, 1994), p. 26.

3. Max Weber, "Geschaftsbericht," *Deutscher Sociologentag, Verhandlungen* 1(1911): 39-62. Quoted by David Sills, "Voluntary Association," in *The International Encyclopedia of Social Science*, 1968, pp. 362-379.

4. In one meeting in October 1992, there were more than half a dozen professional women in the room of fifty members and guests, three dentists, a doctor, two attorneys, and several Certified Public Accountants. A circle of clients for professional service businesses can be built by regular participation. Field Notes, New Jersey Association of Women Business Owners, Middlesex County Chapter Breakfast Meeting, October 19, 1992.

5. Cynthia Fuchs Epstein, "Workplace Boundaries: Conceptions and Creations," *Social Research* 56:3 (Autumn 1989): 571-590. Cynthia Fuchs Epstein, "Tinkerbells and Pinups: The Construction and Reconstruction of Gender Boundaries at Work," In Michele Lamont and Marcel Fournier (eds.) *Cultivating Differences: Symbolic Boundaries and the Making of Inequality* (Chicago: University of Chicago Press, 1991), pp. 232-256.

Gender Identity and Self-positioning

Earlier studies of women and work roles document that women's priorities in self identification according to gender norms vary (Deaux, 1992). Gender, the social definition of differences between males and females, is reflexively maintained through interaction among individuals exercising some choice in their self-interpretations (Deaux, 1987; Epstein, 1992; Goffman, 1959, 1967; Stets and Burke, 1996; West and Zimmerman, 1987).[1] Other referents for personal identity such as class, age or generation also may take precedence in the individual's assessment of social position and personal identity when interacting in business settings. The structure of business and society make gender a basis of social organization. Thus women must negotiate both personal interpretation and social boundaries that guide interaction and the meaning of female gender in our culture.

In business relationships where men have defined cultural styles of negotiation and dominate social interaction, women and men may carry different degrees of power. The power to define the terms of business influences how the individual positions and maneuvers the self within the boundaries of cultural norms (Eagly, 1987; Deaux and LaFrance, 1998).[2] Gender performance is part of self-presentation in business. Self-positioning by individuals is guided by the norms and expectations of interaction in business settings, but such guidelines are interpreted. Self-positioning can be understood as (1) self-definition, the understanding of personal characteristics, values and practices, (2) social identity, defined by the expectations of people interacting within the boundaries of a cultural setting, and (3) strategic self-presentation, an ongoing communication about identity and goals, usually a conscious negotiation of the meaning of individual and collective belonging (Goffman, 1959). As one business woman narrates, all three aspects of identity, self-definition, social identity, and strategic identity coexist in a first meeting with business men.

When I meet men for the first time for an account, let's say, it's like boom, to the point. In some cases, like, "this is who we are. This is what we need. What do you have?" As opposed to approaching an account with a male and seeing the way they interact. It's always a buddy-buddy first and then they blend into business, so there's a difference.

I see them interpreting a woman as being a woman and I think men visualize, not all men but most men, visualize a woman especially in business as one who is a woman. Which they consider weaker, or not as strong to take on what this calls for. That's from one angle. From another angle, sometimes it may be from the male-female approach. So more or less from a sexual point of view. And that I've gotten. So it's almost like you have to be open to any approach and then maneuver yourself in a way that you get what you want.

The men establish "this is who we are," 'can you give us what we need?' Can the woman establish her identity, who she is and what she can give them? The woman is challenged on the point of basic identity. A business meeting includes a moment of truth in which the identity of the business owner must be accepted. There is some possibility for challenging and adapting norms to accommodate changing expectations about gender, because social structure shapes the presentation of self and social attitudes.

Second, the business woman observes that social identity processes between males involve exchanging "buddy-buddy" language, the sharing of cultural and symbolic communication establishing that both sides of the negotiation belong to the same group; social status is gendered. The business woman must deal with the attribution of sexual and social characteristics which exclude her from the interaction, a weaker, sexual person, undermining her claim to deal with the males as an equal.

Third, the business woman must position her "self" in the most advantageous way to gain from the meeting. Being "open to any approach," requires an extra measure of social intelligence, the ability to anticipate uncertain responses, as well as flexibility, the ability to present herself so as to achieve the best outcome from the interaction. Women find "selves" being tested in situations dominated by businessmen.

The act of imagining differences between men and women must be grounded in both experience and ideology. "Buddy-buddy" social identification is supported by beliefs about gender difference, visualizing or imagining, that women are weak. These beliefs then justify discounting or devaluing women's roles in business. Studies have shown that in professions and corporations trust is based on homosocial relationships between men (Jackall, 1989; Kanter, 1978; Lorber, 1994).[3] The opportunity for women to appear as independent actors, with or without a man, in a wide range of trade and market activities challenges traditional business culture, which remains predominantly male. Assumptions about the range of women's business activities have changed slowly, and individuals often use references from their cultural memory to make sense of interactions in business settings that may have an entirely different gender etiquette from the one they grew up with. In the following narrative, the owner of an advertising firm anticipates barriers to women's participation in business based on how she imagines the connection between homosocial male networks of independent business and glass ceiling experiences in corporate employment:

> we can be pushing to get women accepted and to get the old boys network. After J (President of the Middlesex County Chapter) says, "I hate that!," I say, "but it's still out there." I just choose to ignore it . . . these women business owners . . . come from corporate backgrounds. And they just choose to ignore it. I mean if you don't want us, fine. We'll do it and we'll show you who's better. I hate to have that conflict, but that's where it's at. And the pendulum will swing this way and then it swings this way and everybody will end up in the middle and everybody will be equal. Eventually, in a hundred years from now, they're gonna accept it all. And I think that women do need to break through into the corporate world, higher than they have been.

Women in business are aware of how limited levels of information and authority are attributed to their sex. Identity as a business person depends on the individual strategy to both challenge cultural limitations, to "push" individually and collectively, and to achieve normative acceptance, 'just do it, ignore the dissonance, and we will show you who is better.' Despite her experience with sexist male preferences, the woman business owner quoted above believes there has been progress toward gender equality. The perception that 'an old boy network' exists was shaped by prior corporate experience. The conscious separation of association members from male and female dichotomous relations, 'old' networks, is a redefinition of traditional networking strategies based on strategic interaction. NJAWBO members are bringing new wine to old wineskins in part by changing the cultural expectations about who should own and run the vineyard.

The references to "one hundred years from now" do not indicate a blind faith in progress, but reflect the hard work of the women who are trying to achieve success in business. People still assume that association with male lovers, spouses and relatives explain women's business positions. Male dominated industries do not absolutely exclude women, but socially subordinate them. Members of women's associations look for strategies to connect with the larger networks of business relations that are defined by males. They do not assume that gender is the root cause of their disadvantage, but they do encounter men and women who question the managerial role of women in business.

Cynthia Epstein has shown in her studies of telephone company workers that individuals develop investments in boundary distinctions such as masculine, feminine, class and age typed role behavior.[4] While the real boundaries around group categories in our culture change, the conceptual boundaries remain. Erving Goffman's theory (1959) of the self emphasizes how people play social roles defined through interactions in defined settings. Goffman's "self" performs roles on an ongoing interpretive basis, adjusting to the social expectations necessary to maintain the norms of the particular setting. The woman entrepreneur, like her male counterpart, continuously encounters interactions in business settings which require her to maintain an impression of confident and competent business know-how. But women must also maintain a normative performance of femininity without appearing weak when they bargain and trade. The business woman's roles are performed and interpreted among the diverse settings in which she must position her "selves" for advantage. This presents the business woman with challenges as well as opportunities for using the disjuncture between conservative gender ideology and real practices to establish stronger relationships, and thus stronger roles, with others in business.

Members of the New Jersey Association of Women Business Owners try to change the cultural views that the people in their communities hold about women's roles in business. A President in northern New Jersey recounted her experience and goals, which include a strong emphasis on positioning the self in an affirmative and friendly manner:

> I really don't like the she-male, man-haters club. All of us need other peo-
> ple to help us. And other people tend to be really willing to help, if we
> position it properly. I think its really important to take away the barriers
> to people's businesses, so that if you're in construction and you go to a
> construction industry convention, they don't ignore you because you're
> female. I've worked in male dominated businesses before and its worked
> to my advantage. For some reason, they think I'm smarter than they are,
> I don't know why.

In this case, the rarity of a woman in male business environments helped a NJAWBO member to appear smart and exceptional.

The Middlesex County Chapter of NJAWBO offered public seminars in 1992 to increase public awareness about the extent of women's business participation. One of the goals of the Chapter was to challenge notions that women just play at business, by showing that they build good firms which are important to the local economy. As this member of the Middlesex County chapter described, women want to integrate themselves into the community and develop more recognition, prestige and political leverage, thus making the need for a woman's association obsolete.

> One of the goals that we have for our chapter is to become very visible in
> the community.... We provided a seminar for the community. And that

was our fund-raiser because all of the chapters have fund-raisers and some
do card exchanges . . . We didn't want to do that because we didn't want
to be considered female. I know this sounds strange, but our chapter does
not want to be considered women per se; we want to be considered business people....very conscious about being considered business people
instead of the old boy's network, old girls network. We're business people
and we want to take the gender out of it. So one of the things that we
wanted to do was let the community know that we have very successful
people in our group and we don't just sit there knitting and talking about
children and so on. We have professionals; we have a lot of information;
we are a part of the community. We're gonna share it.

The beliefs which control gender as a division of labor reside in the
public perception of women's social roles. Women still must struggle to be
defined as professionals bearing valuable knowledge, and not just as mothers. For NJAWBO members, defining themselves as professionals involves
a conscious and strategic distancing from the limiting norms of past generations of gender ideology which position women in the home amid children
and other domestic concerns.

By increasing recognition and authority in the community, the women
in NJAWBO seek to acquire greater power in the definition of the terms of
their participation in society. NJAWBO members complain that many of
the people they encounter in their public roles perceive their association
events to be new forms of "women's club" activities, and do not see them
as serious forums. People who hold sexist ideas about women's capacities
for business search relentlessly for proof that women limit themselves in
business for rational reasons, or do not have "the right stuff" for success.
The President of the Middlesex NJAWBO chapter in 1992 told me that if
women want to succeed they must, "put their ear muffs on," when other
people challenge their decision to be more than mothers and workers.

It is unclear that either individual or collective strategies to change the
gender boundaries of business can be successful, but frequent activities may
have the latent effect of redefining the expectations of the public and other
market actors. This illustrates the central paradox in women's business
association strategies. NJAWBO members favor gender neutral identities as
'business people.' They join a women's organization in order to overcome
the limits associated with female gender by creating strategies to gender-
integrate business relations. In a study of communications workers, Epstein
found that the decision to emphasize roles and identities in different contexts depended on the individual perception of possibilities for recognition,
status, and value (Epstein, 1988, 1993).[5] For example, working class men
and women who felt limited in their careers emphasized family, friends and
sports activities as important sources of valued personal identities. NJAW-
BO provides a forum in which individuals find support for their identities
as business owners.

The interviews with New Jersey businesswomen show the tensions created when individuals distance themselves from female gender as a unified status category. Many women do not want to belong to a "women's organization." They do not mean to denigrate themselves while they actively challenge the social construction of women's roles. They seek to shift the salience of gender from the general cultural boundaries of public perception to a purely incidental personal characteristic. In the following account, another young woman exhibits a powerful desire for a woman to be seen as a business person, not a "woman," "female," or any specific gender or ethnic signification that might limit "doing business."

> We're not a woman's organization. There's a big difference. There are other women's organizations, they're not the same. There's the American Business Women's Association, I presented to them... let's take out the title here. There are other women's groups, professional women's groups, it's not the same feeling as NJAWBO. The reason is they don't understand when you're trying to meet payrolls and you have to physically call up people to get the checks in to make payrolls. That's not something that they're used to. So it's business owners. So if there are people in the Chamber who are small business owners, I can relate to them because we have the same experiences. I don't really care if you're male/female, if you're black, white, purple or whatever. Professional people don't understand what it's like to be a business owner.

This narrative reveals someone struggling to separate herself and her public identity from the masses of working women who may belong to an association that does not exclude employees. She distances herself from the American Business and Professional Women's Association, an organization which includes support staff employees who have less prestige than managers. The woman I quoted above expresses an awareness of the devaluation of women's work in business, but she wants to break the status devaluation of "women's" organization, as if it did not have to apply to her because she is a business owner. She makes an implicit claim to occupational status privileges, separate from bases of gender solidarity. Class position is the salient focus, based on shared occupational status. The pressures of sexist norms create tensions among women owners to uphold occupational and class-based status distinctions.

Women enter the market at a disadvantage because gender is used as a fundamental basis for social relations. But women entrepreneurs believe that individual strategies for success will have the effect of changing gender segregation, and that they will undercut common assumptions about the differences between men and women. Proving one's intelligence means negotiation within the rules of the market game, despite social and economic disadvantages. Survival as independent business owners proves that women can win a better place for themselves through individual strategies, organizing and negotiating their own lives.

The project of feminism is an analysis of women's status that focuses attention on collective subordination. Women are encouraged to understand themselves as limited subjects, positioned by dominant others (males or male defined classes) through existing social structures in ways that can only be surmounted by direct challenge and protest. A market oriented feminism challenges sexist gender norms in business by creating identities for women as independent deal makers with power over the management of their firms. The market self is an activist on behalf of individual self-interest. Liberal individualism thus appears to be liberating because women do not have to focus their attention on collective disadvantages; every women should pursue opportunity and even advantage based on her individual resources.

Market feminists emphasize active mediation, building a better life for the individual, and improving opportunities for women's collective participation in business, politics and all areas of civic life. The incentives for embracing the market as a source of strategies and role models for women's emancipation include control over the labor process, satisfaction in achievement of a deal through offering a quality product or service, and acquiring the market value for what one produces instead of only a wage. To pursue market based strategies, the individual must ignore social limitations, which are a strong source of cognitive dissonance, as well as commentators on subordination, while pushing forward with what she believes will work to support an independent living in the world. Proving one's intelligence means successfully negotiating the structures and the relationships of the capitalist world as they exist. Individual business women are continuously challenging their social limitations. It is ironic that in the face of this dynamism by boundary challengers, the market feminist solution undermines the legitimacy of feminist politics, because capitalism maintains stratification patterns which privilege some women over others, embedded in class and cultural distinctions. Entrepreneurial individuals rising in the middle classes and sometimes within elite family networks, must establish social identities in relationships with male businessmen, and privilege those relationships over alternative ideals.

CONSERVING GENDER IDENTITY

In their expectations about human behavior, both men and women preserve beliefs in gender differences, even as they face changing opportunities for social action. Contemporary gender roles combine innovations derived from traditional expectations with women's perceived experience as active organizers of their own lives. Women or men may transport children to day care, but women still perform a second shift of housework and family care after the paid working day (Hochschild, 1989). Women business owners adapt ideas that help them to organize personal gender identity in the context of their changing economic and social roles, as well as their changing expectations for an increased range in their participation in market relations. The owner of a regional human resources management corporation defines her role as that of a helping professional, in providing an important function for families:

> ...I'm still a very helping professional. I change people's lives here. I've had women crying in the chair - thank you, you've taken me off of welfare. Thank you for finding me a job. Even that's not what I do. I don't find people jobs. I really help the client find the right person. I still have changed people's lives. ...we relocate professionals and you would think, oh, well that's not a big deal. I've had people send us notes. I've had grandmothers call me that say, thank you for finding my son, bringing him back... we really, truly affect families. And we affect companies. So it's really a helping profession.

> In fact I heard a woman say once to me, and I really identify with this, for a woman her business is like you can equate that with a child. She would not want to give up that child ever. You could do anything to that woman but she wouldn't give up her child. Well, the same could be said for women business owners. You could do anything to that woman but she's not going to give up her business.

This corporation owner valued being viewed as someone who cared about the people she placed as temporary and permanent staff on the East coast. She defined herself as a helping professional who changed people's lives, rather than as the Chief Executive Officer of a medium size corporation with respectable growth and profits from head-hunting and employee leasing. She actively adapts her market activities and professional role to the normative cultural value of females expressing "caring," an ideological concept.

In the following narrative a 28-year old, upper middle class woman, who started her business following a brief period of employment after college, expresses several possible strategies for her future life, as a wife, a mother, a politician, a volunteer, and an entrepreneur, all of which coexist in a flux of possible identities, desires and goals that may be combined in the reconstruction of life.

> I'm looking more at the big picture when I date somebody. And I know that now I'm still 27 but I still have time to have children. But in 10 years I'll be 37 so, hopefully I'll have kids by then. And as far as a career, that totally depends on probably the person I marry. Because what I really, really want to do is volunteer full time. I would like to get into political office a little bit. Maybe on local town councils. And I'd also like to be

able to volunteer full time wherever it ends up being.... if I do end up marrying someone who has enough to be able to support us and a family, that's ... what I want to do. But if I don't that's fine too. The next career that I'd like to look into for myself would be owning a child care center, or doing something with children. Mostly likely a nursery or day care, something like that.

These women are maintaining and producing female gender identity by adapting idealized traditional values such as caring, helping and nurturing, in both their narratives and practice of commercial enterprise. Gender identity is being maintained through interaction as a positional preference of the individual women I interviewed. They hold essentialist beliefs and ideologies about womanhood, rooting their practices in care giving and motherhood. Thus, they position themselves through their choices, and how they imagine possibilities for their future. There are myths of idealized practices in the culture's past, selfless full time motherhood, and public recognition tied to volunteer work beyond the pecuniary interests of the market. Their ambition and market participation are woven into the normative cultural values and practices that they express in their narratives.

Few women would accept the dependency and lack of control over decision making that the old ideals and expectations of domesticity would entail. But the language and ideology of a modern, publicly active, "true womanhood" still exist, actively adapted to new conditions and experiences. Entrepreneurs appropriate elements of culture, beliefs and practices about the roles of women and the role of entrepreneur, without completely accepting the ideology and social controls that enforce the separation of domestic and economic spheres. Cultural references in the social dialogue regarding the traditional roles of "womanhood" function to maintain social relationships by reassuring everyone that the individual still performs a genuine and sincere "female" self through her public business activities.

Association advocates have embraced some essentialist assumptions about gender differences. These essentialist perspectives set up a false contrast between men and women who are embedded in the same economic and cultural structures, largely in reaction to women's perceived disadvantage in the face of ongoing sexism. The female difference model can be interpreted as a source of social power that men want to emulate, or at least accept as a valuable style of management. In a press release titled, "New Study Quantifies Thinking and Management Differences Between Women and Men Business Owners," NFWBO reports the findings of a research study underwritten by American Express Small Business Services, which strongly reinforces essentialist beliefs that men and women are biologically different.

More than half of women owners (53%) emphasize intuitive or "right brain" thinking. This style stresses creativity, sensitivity and values-based decision making. Seven out of ten (71%) men business owners emphasize logical or "left-brain" thinking. This style stresses analysis, processing information methodically and developing procedures. Women business owners' decision making is more "whole-brained" than their male counterparts, that is, more evenly distributed between right and left brain thinking.

The study measures how deeply men and women believe that gender differences are innate rather than socially constructed. Popular sexist explanations for male and female differences are rationalized as scientific facts, which have social consequences insofar as they influence public policy, individual decision making and the behavior and assumptions of people doing business. Laura Henderson, 1994 Chair of the National Foundation for Women Business Owners, stressed the companionate marriage of male and female differences:

> Up to now, models for business success have been largely male-defined, often forcing women into a mold in which they did not feel comfortable. The recognition that both women and men's styles of success will help them both strengthen their management styles and learn from each other.[6]

The woman responsible for the following quote serves on the national board of the National Foundation for Women Business Owners. She does not want to give up a potential advantage of traditional claims to female difference:

> ... an industry where you need the strong sensitivity to people that we as women tend to develop early in life where men don't always develop it, ...people still.... have the tendency to lean toward men as advisors because of former experience or whatever reason. However, ...one of the reasons I see our business doing so well is that's changing. You see it in the corporate world because now men are starting to want to be like women and be nurturing and participate in management styles and all of those things that historically women have been that have not been a positive thing, that have been viewed as a negative. Today that's no longer true ...I'm getting more and more men who would prefer to deal with a woman because they see women as being caring and concerned about them as individuals and not just looking at the numbers. In my industry, I think that some of the things that women are facing today are positive versus negative. I think we're gaining ground rapidly because of the way we're being viewed as a positive influence in people's lives which I think is great.

The shift in the interpretation of gender differences between men and women is an outcome of social and cultural politics, deliberate strategies and ideas designed to engage the imaginations and belief systems of the public. Most people are not innovators, but adopters of styles or strategies that have already been accepted by a significant number of people. The belief that men and women are essentially different can control behavior.

The National Foundation For Women Business Owners proselytize the acceptance and recognition of gender differences between men and women, not as a protest, but as a traditional claim to moral and emotional difference from men as a basis for power and respect. Both sexes are reassured that the new "entrepreneurial woman" is not a threat to the normative cultural construction of masculine and feminine gender differences. One difficulty created by this cultural politics strategy is the reinforcement of male and female behavioral norms supporting cultural boundaries which have historically disadvantaged women in economic exchange activities, by positioning women as more emotional, and thus too weak to compete with dispassionate, masculine businessmen. Beliefs thus create contradictions between how some women interpret gender and how they seek rationalized equality in a public quest to become managerial leaders.

WOMEN LOOKING BACKWARD, LOOKING FORWARD

Deaux and Major (1987) show that critical life events may alter the hierarchy one assigns various identities such as gender, age or marital status, to make them more or less central at different times.[7] Four women describe their life experiences as generational or referenced to age, which effects how gender roles are interpreted in their lives:

> Well it started really in the late '60s, I remember hearing about careers in some grade school, and this exposure, just things changing and listening to your parents and seeing that lifestyle. You laugh and look back at the shows you used to watch, women in the aprons, just the perfect "wife." And you look at what you know, and some of it's bad, the divorce rate and all that, but I definitely think it had a major impact on a lot of women being raised almost in that turning stage. From what was traditionally thought to be the correct way and then what the opportunities that we were being told by the women's movement.....I was born in 1956. I'll be 37 in a few months....

> I think that because I was raised in the '70s, and it was no longer the way women were raised in the '50s and '60s. You were getting raised just to be mommies and find yourself a husband. I think that whole experience in the late '60s and early '70s and being exposed to a different mind set for me, as well as a lot of my other friends. So we went on to do things that weren't so limited, although we did do the traditional thing, get married and have children. That wasn't our whole life. We had another agenda that we had to accomplish, and we all kind of did it in our own separate ways. So that was the individual part.

if you want to point a finger and say - woman - it could have been that. I'm not going to say that because I don't know if that's so true or not. But I was young. I had a limited amount of experience in starting a business. And even though I did make it successful that didn't mean anything. There wasn't enough there. I didn't have any collateral. I rented. I rented an apartment. I leased my car.... I was young. I didn't own a house. I mean they [the bank] couldn't [loan me money]. . .

I was probably in my early 30's and I think at that time most women change anyway, you become more secure or confident. The more you do the more you know, the more aggressive you can be as far as going after certain things. I think it had a combination to do with having the responsibility of making a business work and also maturing.

In the following narrative, an exporter interprets how women at different ages try to make sense out of their choices.

Someone said that they're going back to the traditional things, the values. Someone was telling me that her daughter isn't of age and they're looking for the secure way, the traditional way and they want to get married. Although they're going to college their primary goals are almost going back to what we thought about. We're not going to get married and we're going to do this and do that. And have our own lives. I've heard that shift too and it's kind of scary, because the women who came of age in the '70s built careers and had children. And a lot of the women who are coming of age now, and are in their early twenties seem to think that they can't do both or that the conservative older model is somehow better, more secure. But the opportunities for doing that have really shrunk because it is harder to make a living period. And both people have to work. And it's harder to find a good job period.

I think though maybe that some of these girls that saw their mother struggle doing both and that's why they think they have the opportunity not to struggle and not to have to go through so much. Of course anyone would rather not if they don't have to, so maybe that's why they're looking at it differently.

References to generation, work experience, and dreams of the future indicate that women experience changes in the self that are not specifically gendered. Women refer to psychological "take charge" changes in their selves such as confidence, feeling positive, finding a sense of power or a strength.

I don't know if changing would be the word. I would say I felt myself feeling more comfortable with myself and growing and being able to be myself even more. If anything I was more of an introvert, so doing the business and networking and meeting new people and starting almost like a new phase of my life, caused me to be open and know that I could still trust and talk to people... the things I was experiencing on a personal level and on a business level.

Epstein (1995) reports finding similar responses among women attorneys employed by large law firms in New York City. She reports that these women refer to changes such as becoming more analytical, more in control; these qualities are noticed in their personal lives and experiences as well.[8] Women may also be aware of changes in the self that are caused by increased levels of responsibility, over-identification with the business and stress. This can lead to an acute self-consciousness, which this young corporation owner experiences:

the thing is that when you have your own business you're always thinking about it. When you're on vacation you're thinking oh, there's somebody I might be able to do a job for. I'll go talk with them. . . . it is your life. It's not like you can separate yourself from it. So mentally you're always working on it. All the time. I would say that I spent every waking moment talking and planning my business. I'm a very driven person. I think about business when I'm in the shower. I'm a little neurotic. That's why I started laughing at you when I said, Oh, you're going to have fun in NJAWBO. Because we're all a little neurotic.

Men are expected to be committed to their work, placing their professional identities before all else. For women, identification with business may be a new aspect of self understanding, leading individuals to joke about their "neurotic" obsession, a characterization that would not occur to the average businessman.

Individuals exercise some choice in their interpretations of gender roles and signify both their social structural position and their personal identities within changing cultural boundaries. Individuals interpret gender by combining innovations in roles derived from traditional expectations, with the experience of actively organizing of their own lives. This makes it possible for women and men to adapt women's changing roles into the normative structures of business and society while maintaining gender differentiation as a basis for social structure.

CHAPTER NOTES

1. Kay Deaux, "Psychological Constructions of Masculinity and Femininity." In *Masculinity/Femininity: Basic Perspectives*, June M. Reinisch, L. Rosenblum and S. Sanders (eds.) (New York: Oxford University Press, 1987), pp. 289-303; Cynthia Fuchs Epstein, "Tinker bells and Pin-ups: The Construction and Reconstruction of Gender Boundaries at Work." In M. Lamont and M. Fourier (eds.) *Cultivating Differences: Symbolic Boundaries and the Making of Inequality* (Chicago: University of Chicago Press, 1989); Erving Goffman, *The Presentation of Self in Everyday Life* (New York: Doubleday Books, 1959), and *Interaction Ritual* (New York: Anchor Books, 1967); Jan E. Stets and Peter J. Burke, "Gender, Control and Interaction," *Social Psychological Quarterly* 59, 3 (1996): 193-220; Candace West and Don H. Zimmerman, "Doing Gender," *Gender and Society* 1 (1987): 125-151.

2. Alice H. Eagly, *Sex Differences in Social Behavior: A Social-Role Interpretation* (Hillsdale, NJ: Erlbaum Associates, 1987); Kay Deaux and Marianne Lafrance, "Gender," Chapter Seventeen, in Daniel T. Gilbert, Susan Fiske and Gardner Lindzey (eds.) *The Handbook of Social Psychology, Vol. One*, Fourth edition (New York: Oxford University Press and McGraw Hill, 1998), pp. 788-827.

3. Rosabeth Moss Kanter, *Men and Women of the Corporation* (New York: Basic Books, 1977); Judith Lorber, *Paradoxes of Gender* (New Haven: Yale University Press).

4. Cynthia Fuchs Epstein, "Workplace Boundaries: Conceptions and Creations," *Social Research* 56, 3 (Autumn 1989), p. 573.

5. Cynthia Fuchs Epstein, *Deceptive Distinctions: Sex, Gender and the Social Order* (New haven: Yale University Press, 1988); C. F. Epstein, *Women In Law* (Urbana: University of Illinois Press, 1993).

6. National Foundation For Women Business Owners. (1994, July 19). Press Release. New Study Quantifies Thinking and Management Differences Between Women and Men Business-Owners [Online]. Available at http//www.nfwbo.org/rr003.htm [July 8, 1997].

7. Kay Deaux and Brenda Major, "Putting Gender Into Context: An Interactive Model of Gender-related Behavior," *Psychological Review*, 94 (1987), pp. 369-389.

8. Cynthia Fuchs Epstein, "The Difference Model: Enforcement and Reinforcement of Women's Roles In Law," in Judith Blau and Norman Goodman (eds.) *Social Roles and Social Institutions: Essays in Honor of Rose Laub Coser* (New Brunswick, NJ: Transaction Publishers, 1995).

Managing Employees

Contrary to claims that women lead and manage in a different way than males (Helgesen, 1989; Godfrey, 1992; Rosener, 1990), a number of social psychologists have established that women and men do not differ in their leadership styles, which are structured by managerial work roles (Eagly and Johnson, 1990). But in laboratory experiments in which individuals act upon their beliefs rather than real role demands, and in assessment studies of individuals who are not being considered for leadership in management roles, participants confirmed gender stereotypical behavior (Eagly and Johnson, 1990). While women employers confront the same problems that any employer would face, they sometimes stereotype their own behavior, "women's" behavior," or refer to cultural frameworks that use the "family" as a source of role models. Deeply held ideological beliefs about differences between men and women can shape individual narratives and self-reports.

When asked if women are more cooperative, empathetic, caring, less autocratic, or dictatorial, men and women responding to surveys claim they manage in different styles because of their gender. Judith Rosener reported in the *Harvard Business Review* (1990) that women executives and business owners shared a special "women's style." Women managers reported exhibiting empathy, trust, sharing and caring in their relationships with employees.[1] My observations and interviews with members of the New Jersey Association of Women Business Owners and other women entrepreneurs in the tri-state region, confirm that women's interpretations of their roles shape the way they narrate the practice of management. But these same individuals hold diverse management practices that they adapted to the structural demands of operating a small business. While narration and practice are related, if women exhibit sex-typed characteristics as small business owners, these characteristics are rooted in cultural constructions of gender and ideological beliefs, not universal or essential practices.

MANAGING WORK ROLES

The primary concern of all small business owners is control over the labor process, including quality, timeliness and consistency. Business owners not only wish to control their own time, they must control the time and behavior of their workers. The workplace conditions structuring entrepreneurial managerial roles reflect small employers interacting with workers within the constraints and resources of close, interpersonal work regimes. Most of the women interviewed for this study employ fewer than five workers. This finding is close to the *1987 Census of Women Owned Businesses* data (U.S. Department of Commerce, 1987). The following table illustrates the micro-employer distribution among women interviewed for this study.

The owner decides who to hire, what to sell, prices, wages and organi-

TABLE 8. NUMBER OF EMPLOYEES AMONG WOMEN OWNERS		
Number of Employees	1987 Census	Study Sample '92-'93
<5 Employees	78%	80% (28)
5-9 Employees	13%	11% (4)
10>	9%	9% (3)

1987 Census of Women Owned Businesses N = 3,102,685.
Sample N=35

zation. She must decide who contributes to her business and what the standards of that contribution will be. Workers and owners interact with one another in a close and detailed way, usually on a daily basis. In small businesses, management styles reflect more interpersonal control strategies. Granovetter (1984) also found that the size of a firm is a significant structural condition in relationships between workers and managers in small businesses. He writes:

> That many workers enter small firms through contacts reinforces the likelihood that workers in such firms are in an environment structured more by personal relationships than by bureaucratic procedures.[2]

Becoming employers causes women to take on authoritative roles as managers. The position of owner as manager, not the sex of the person, causes the individual to use interpersonal and professional strategies suited to small firms. Women owners have several strategies for control over the labor process. The first strategy is to give their employees responsibility for solving problems and offering ideas about work and service delivery. The second strategy is to emphasize the functional interdependency of everyone working in the small firm, which business owners often characterize as a family. A third strategy is subcontracting to home-based workers, using leased workers, part time help, immigrants and people working off the books. A fourth strategy is managerial distance, duplicating the boundaries the owner learned while working for a larger corporation.

The owner manager in the following quotation exhibits the first strategy. She motivates her employees by emphasizing their responsibility to the success of the work process:

> I'm demanding. So my perfect employee is somebody absolutely wholly committed to making this company grow. Wholly and completely committed. Now that's a lot to ask from somebody. It really truly is. But I've been very fortunate that I motivate these people to want to do that. And when somebody isn't wholly and completely committed to the company, I've let them go. I'm really tough to work for. I'm not an easy person to work for. I've said, okay, well your time is up here. You're not putting everything into it anymore. I don't like 'hanger-oners'. I want people that are always going to come up with ideas . . . what can we do for this client? We're going to make it better. I don't want people just spending time here.

Employees are encouraged to recognize their responsibility as problem solvers. The negotiation of power between the owner-manager and staff appears egalitarian because all of the participants judge each other's performance. But the ultimate authority to fire individuals is retained by the owner, who keeps a close watch on daily interactions in the business. Interactions are personal because there is no intervening system of rules and status levels to mediate between the owner and the worker. Trust is based on looking at the employee rather than evaluating a sheaf of paper in a personnel file.

Small employers like to define their employees as a second family who work in harmony. This works well if employees invest their emotions in a primary dependency relationship. The family is a model for the employer-employee relationship in which employees are expected to develop emotional commitments to the business and the owner. The three owner-managers below acknowledge their interdependency with employees, which means that each individual must create interpersonal trust in her interactions.

> Basically we're a team. Our people are friends, family. They're all part of a team and we all work together. And you have to trust them. That's the major thing is that you really have to be able to trust them because you don't have the kind of control systems that you have in the corporate world, so you can't double check everything, and you can't follow behind people because you just don't have time to do that.

It's like a family, it really is. Because we know that it's unrealistic to say don't bring your personal problems into it because they'll come into it anyway. So if somebody has something they have to deal with, we have to help them deal with it so they can stop thinking about it and focus on the business.

Well, we have a very relaxed way of doing things. I've worked for people who, the moment you walk through their door you felt the tension. And we're not like that. We're very relaxed. We want to create a sort of family atmosphere. People who work for us feel comfortable. Our clients feel comfortable.

Control over workers in the small firm operates through personal commitments. Retirees, young mothers, and displaced workers fit the social face of the second family metaphor, which portrays them as working in a "caring" environment.

We have one person who's been with us the longest who we hired through an ad in the paper. ....One lady was a client. She wanted to retire and work part-time, so I hired her. Another lady was a friend through another organization. Another was a sister-in-law of a good friend of mine. So primarily through word of mouth, through friends or people that we know which is what we prefer to do. We have a tendency to hire people that are retired, returning to the work force or career change kinds of people who are older with experience.

The emphasis on lady-like friendship voiced by this businesswomen symbolically compensates the worker for the lower pay and uncertain employment in the small business sector. By offering trust and respect for employees with diverse work histories, she retains their loyalty. Pringle's (1988) study of secretaries also found that close personal relationships were the small business manager's strongest source of control over the secretary's performance.[3]

Not all women employers refer to their employees as their "family," friends, or consider them to be their equals. Nor should they be expected to do so. The use of sexist language and stereotyping to signal power and dominance in relationships with employees is consistent with the use of the family as a metaphor for managerial relationships. Gender ideology traditionally positions the male owner-manager above the feminized staff person. Women owners sometimes assume styles of authority and power that are associated with male roles. The following quote from a female employer of two full time and two part time women employees expresses a subordinate definition of the support staff person:

It's more than personality. Because the gal with the right attitude, the gal with that helpful, honest attitude . . . I don't think anything else works.

The use of the word "gal" explicitly reinforces the female employee's subordinate status. The cultural equation of sexist language and managerial language complicates the analysis of gender as a unitary category.

Although I did not ask about the gender distribution among employees, I observed that sixteen out of thirty-five business owners employed all women, with an average of two employees. With forty-six percent of the sample engaged in same-sex employment patterns, this partially confirms the argument that women's entrepreneurship is being sustained by women organizing other women at the bottom of the wage scale (Beechey, 1987; Bluestone and Kuhn, 1987; Rubery, 1989).[4] Women share a set of meanings about 'what women are like,' and tend to reward or punish individuals for performing according to the group's expectations about gender differences. There may be a greater variety of shared norms among small firms because the beliefs of the owner determine the composition of the firm and what behaviors are tolerated or discouraged in small scale cultures of the workplace. Micro firm cultures may be liberating individuals from the straight jackets of traditional male and female gender roles, but among these micro cultures there are also people reinforcing cultural beliefs that reaffirm gender differences.

A woman who is a small employer may have more in common with other small employers than she does with women who are her workers. Some women even hold a preference for interacting with males. The two owners below reveal how some women owners may have negative feelings toward women based on assumptions about women's traditional roles:

I work with men, and I just react to people and their personalities. And I get along better with some than others. Women can be very, very difficult to deal with. Women executives can be extremely difficult because some of them are what I call piranhas. It's not like men executives. They're so uptight and proving, or whatever this personality is that's pushed them up there, and it's not just a matter of being tough, they really do want to chew you up and spit you out, and I'd just assume not work with them.

Twice I had women who worked for me, hired them as typists—I used to call them Stepford wives. They wouldn't think. If it wasn't written down exactly, they couldn't figure it out. They couldn't open a folder to figure out that it should be done this way. They didn't want to understand it. They didn't want to learn. They didn't want to grow. They didn't want to do anything. They just wanted to sit there and type whatever I said, exactly the way I said it. And if I didn't say it and implied it, it didn't get done right. It drove me crazy. I need someone who can work independently because I cannot stand over them. I'm not a mother, and I'm tired of teaching.

Women are not just the objects of stereotyping by males. They may also stereotype themselves and other women (Epstein, 1988, 1993). Working for a woman in a small business does not guarantee that her attitudes toward authority and gender will be more feminist or more egalitarian, even with increased interaction.

Paying personal attention to staff can be a burden for an owner-manager, as a woman from this study reports below:

> Maybe because I'm busy at meetings or something I won't see them (employees). But I actually go to their desks and say how are you doing. And, "what's going on today?" And that could be a drawback or that can be advantageous. It can be a drawback because then you hear about all the garbage too. That other stuff. And because I am very open and everything else, they think that they can come and tell me everything.

Another woman reports that her employees' solutions usually fail, but she tolerates their efforts to solve problems in the interest of good management.

> I do seek out their solutions to certain things. I will let them try things even though I think that it will fail. And it usually does. And I don't say anything. They come back to me and say oh this isn't working, let's do it this way. I let them find the solutions. And I always say to them, don't come to me with a problem, come to me with a couple of solutions. I don't want to hear about the problems. I want to hear about the solutions.

When the owner-manager places her employee in the role of problem solver, the new position of the employee changes the role of the manager. Their ability to perform with minimal supervisory control in a small scale setting, is a measure of managerial success in the small firm, because it frees both worker and manager from wasting time on other kinds of control and oversight strategies.

As an example of the fourth management strategy, I found that a small owner may organize her business according to impersonal managerial and subordinate roles such as the ones she learned as an employee in a corporation. Through the individual's socialization in corporate work settings, a need for rational and impersonal rules may be deeply ingrained. In the following quotation, a broker admits that management requires social distance from her employee:

> You want this nice tight little family unit, but we're not a family. I'm an employer. She's an employee, and there are times when there are going to be differences, so to maintain that objectivity is important.

Status distinctions allow the internal relationships in the firms to function as wage-based and goal oriented. References to the workers' personal characteristics refer to their reliability, not a surrogate family paternalism that might cloud the owner manager's role. In the following quote an office services provider defines her firm as an extension of the corporate client's environment:

> We try to assist and reduce overtime, overhead, eliminate any supervision necessary, so we get to know your product so that we can handle it on our premises and in a sense really what we try to do is become an extension of an existing staff. So that's basically the service we provide.

In the following account, a former manager with the Bell System in New Jersey set a limit on the kind of work she asked of her employees in a shared office suite. She wanted to maintain the value attached to their skill levels:

> I don't like to do that (mailing lists) because that's what I call gorilla work. And I pay people who are a little above gorillas so I like to have them do work that is more suitable to their skills.

The instrumental extension of the corporate manager's techniques into the world of self-employment and small shop supervision, is a vulnerable position, socially and emotionally, because the income and authority levels of the outsourced service vendor never achieve the security and status of large corporate management. Former corporate managers adapt their knowledge and skills to operate businesses in smaller and less secure markets. They face both practical and emotional challenges when they organize to meet the needs and demands of diverse clients.

OTHER STRUCTURAL ISSUES: WAGES AND INSURANCE

In another management strategy, I found women entrepreneurs hire subcontractors and casual part time workers because they cannot guarantee the amount of work they may receive. A client contracts with the owner for a service, and the owner in turn subcontracts with part time workers, a process which the entrepreneur below describes:

> I have what I call independent contractors. ...these individuals work at home. And the typical scenario is I may get maybe four projects in; I know I can probably handle one or two. I'll call maybe Gail; I'll say, "Gail, what's your schedule like?" She's a mother, raising a daughter, and these are the types of individuals I've been able to get as well because they like to stay within the market, stay up on their skills and at the same time they want to raise a family and really have a home life. That's what I was talking about regarding having the flexibility of doing that with the business. ...individuals that I've interviewed, when I explained the concept, it's just

so different, and it's so enlightening that they are ready to accept anything for pay, as low as it can get, do anything they can.

Employees who find the concept of flexibility "enlightening" consent to the social organization of the owner's bargain. This woman did not specify how low wages in the subcontracting market might fall. At the time of this interview in 1992, workers were being paid $7.00 an hour for home based, "outsourced" typing, organized by the business service provider for a large corporation. Contract work is not steady; the acceptance of single projects entails sporadic and uncertain income for the home base worker. The home based worker has control over the scheduling of her own hours within the demands of the contract, but the owner who organizes the project controls the employee by making more or less work available according to the individual's attitude and performance. The word processor, typist, designer web worker or programmer, is expected to be enthusiastic, fast and grateful to the subcontractor. While the amount of work available is uncertain in subcontracting situations, workers themselves may also take other jobs. The personal expressions of commitment to the job by these workers becomes one of the few indexes of workplace control that the owner possesses.

Regular in-house employers, with employees on site, are concerned about the cost of health benefits. A large part of the structural bind for the small employer is the cost of health insurance. The average yearly cost of health benefits in New Jersey in 1993 was $4,297. 00 per employee, equal to 13% of reported average wages.[5] Small employers pay $500 more per employee to cover their workers using conventional health insurance plans, because Health Maintenance Organizations do not cover groups with fewer than 10 employees. They are trapped in a tightening vice-grip of rising health insurance costs and small margins of profit in competitive conditions. The New Jersey Business and Industry Association received 2,000 responses to a survey in 1993 of 13,500 member companies. Eighty percent of respondents were small companies with fewer than 50 employees. This survey reports that 75% of companies with between 1 and 19 employees pay 91-100% of the cost of health insurance; employees pay 1-10%.[6] Roughly 81% of companies with between between 1 and 19 employees provided some health insurance. Owners and employees frequently share the same level of benefits. Eight-seven percent of all businesses provided some health care insurance coverage. The remaining 13% provided no coverage. Among companies with 20 to 49 employees, 96% provided coverage, and 99% of companies with 50 or more employees provided coverage.[7] A National Association of Women Business Owners survey in 1996, found that among the 1,071 women responding, 84% offer one or more benefits to their employees, including some health insurance. This is slightly higher than the percentage for all businesses in the smallest employer category. Women owners strongly believe that their employees should be covered, but it is financially difficult to maintain full health insurance benefits, including major medical, hospitalization, and at least HMO physician coverage, because of this disadvantage in economies of scale

Small employers have options beside paying for major medical. They can require their employees to pay for all or part of their benefits. They can fail to offer benefits. Some firms that employ small numbers of workers have scaled back the commitment to insurance or they have moved to employee leasing, a form of long term temporary employment. At NJAW-BO meetings influential active members sell employee leasing services to small business owners, promoting an option that might otherwise not appeal to the populist small holder's desire for close control over her business. The woman I interviewed below reluctantly reports that she is moving to a leasing system as a way to reduce her health care expenses:

> I'm going to pursue ...employee leasing because then they can get a benefit package put together for them that is more reasonably priced. More reasonably priced than I could get. And I can contribute what I can afford to that as a billing addition. And it will enable us to have benefits and be a little more competitive in terms of what we can offer our employees. But I can't afford to do it on my own. The reason that employee leasing works out well is because it breaks it down into weekly increments which I can afford a lot better than paying out $7,000 at a time for somebody's major medical plan.

As the cost of health care coverage rises, small employers are pushed to either reduce their coverage or look for more casual subcontracting relationships, including home based workers, temporary and leased workers.

Apart from the home based and temporary groups of workers, non-union labor and immigrant labor can also provide a cost savings for businesses. One woman owner praises immigrant workers, while another woman damns unions for creating high wage competition:

> The Spanish community - they're wonderful people. They work hard. They work harder. And I hate to say this, but they work harder than anybody else, any other group that I know of. Because they want to work. And you know what? They don't understand the laws. They don't understand what they're entitled to. So they don't even go apply to half the stuff that they would be entitled to. You know, we have these people here that can only speak Spanish and that's it. And they don't understand that they're entitled to welfare. And they don't understand that they're entitled to unemployment. And they don't understand there is this stuff. And it's a real hassle for them to go and apply for those kinds of things. So they just don't. So what do they do? They work. They work hard. They come here. They say to me, you have work today? Let me work, let me work. And you know what, when I send them on a job they show up. They don't

walk off the job. They do a good job. They're happy. I don't understand this entitlement feeling that people run around having.

We lost one of our supervisors to go work at a local company where he was getting almost double the amount. He's getting paid $16 [per hour]. To take boxes from one place and put them in another place 'cause he's union. Just to take a box to take from one location to another location, and he's getting almost twice. And then if he gets overtime, he's making more than people who are professionals. It's crazy. Because it's a union job. Now I have a major problem with that.

Firms with under fifty employees are rarely organized into the existing union local structure. Unionized firms compete with the small firms for better workers, and many owners oppose the imposition of union wage scales as "customary wages" in job bids in New York City and New Jersey. Owners fiercely oppose raises in the minimum wage.

Women owners derive legitimacy by referring to "business" dilemmas they share with owner-managers in general, expressing stronger class solidarity rather than gender solidarity, but beliefs about gender do shape their narrative assumptions and the terms of their relationships with employees. The majority of owners look to one another to understand how competition shapes wages and benefits. If the firms next door in the same industry offers seven dollars per hour, others must offer less than seven dollars to underbid them. Owners with businesses of similar size encounter the same structural conditions in markets. Wages and benefits are "flexible" insofar as their costs can be kept low. The management strategies of small business owners depend on developing relationships with employees which are characterized according to the values of the owner, as personal relationships or a second family, or as instrumental managerial relationships, but they must do so within existing economic and social boundaries. The demands of entrepreneurial work roles are more important in the structure of social relations between employers and employees than beliefs supporting gender role stereotypes. Nonetheless, belief systems about gender differences matter in how individual women interpret their roles as managers and their relationships with employees. Outside the constraints of real work roles, such as communicating goals about scheduling and production, individuals act upon their beliefs about male and female gender differences, making those beliefs a salient focus for self-reported behavior.

CHAPTER NOTES

1. Judy Rosener, "Ways Women Lead," *Harvard Business Review*, 68 (November-December 1990), pp.119-125.

2. Mark Granovetter, " Small is Bountiful: Labor Markets and Establishment Size," *American Sociological Review* 49 (June 1984), p. 333.

3. Rosemary Pringle, *Secretaries Talk: Sexuality, Power and Work* (New York: Verso, 1988).

4. Veronica Beechey, *Unequal Work* (London: Verso, 1987); Barry Bluestone & Sarah Kuhn, "Economic Restructuring and the Female Labor Market," In L. Beneria and C. Stimpson (eds.) *Women, Households and the Economy*, (New Brunswick, NJ: Rutgers University Press, 1987); Jill Rubery, "Labor Market Flexibility in Britain," In Green, F. (ed.), *Restructuring the British Economy*, (UK: Harvester-Wheatsheaf, 1989).

5. New Jersey Business and Industry Association, "1993 Health Benefits Survey," January 26, 1994, p. 1.

6. New Jersey Business and Industry Association, "1993 Health Benefits Survey," January 26, 1994, Table No. 3.

7. New Jersey Business and Industry Association Press Release, *BIA News*, January 26, 1994, Trenton, NJ.

Family and Household Support

One of the ongoing interests of scholars in the United States since the late 1960's is women's increased participation in permanent full time employment and the organization of motherhood (Parsons, 1951; Epstein, 1988; Hochschild, 1989; Lorber, 1994).[1] The ability to sustain multiple roles and to benefit from diverse experiences is one of the liberating but challenging aspects of contemporary working women's lives (Crosby, 1987, 1993; Coser, 1991; Epstein, 1987, 1997).[2] Middle class women who own businesses in New Jersey may also encounter a range of social stresses and uncertainties over the courses of their lives, including debt, divorce, downsizing, single headed households, co-habitation, and remarriage.

I found that for the business owners, their careers are primary sources of identity as well as a way of insuring their living and the security of their children. Paid or contractual work and reproductive labor such as child rearing and housework are not considered to be mutually exclusive. To nurture and supervise their children, women employ baby sitters, nannies, day care centers, and the volunteer efforts of relatives to relieve them from some of the burdens of domesticity. The family is also a source of credit, capital and emotional support that is highly valued by women.

Among the fifteen women who are mothers in the study sample, both the median and the average number of children is two.

TABLE 9. NUMBER OF CHILDREN AMONG MOTHERS

Number of Children	15 Mothers
1 One	13% (2)
2 Two	53% (8)
3 Three	20% (3)
4 Four	13% (2)
5+ Five of More Children	0%

The average age of their offspring is twenty-four years old, with a range of two to thirty-seven years.[3] Only fourteen of the nineteen mothers reported their age. The average was fifty years old, with a range of thirty-three to sixty-four years. Although there were three women with school age children under age seventeen, most of the mothers made the decision to open a business when their children were in their mid teens or older. Teen age children are more self-reliant, and require less direct supervision; they can independently negotiate their own schedules. The characteristics of the three young mothers is summarized in the following table:

TABLE 10. MOTHERS OF SCHOOL AGE CHILDREN			
CHARACTERISTICS	MOTHER ONE	MOTHER TWO	MOTHER THREE
Age in 1992	33	37	37
Marital Status	Married	Married	Divorced
Number of Children	2	2	3
Age of Children	5, 1.5	4,6	17, 15, 11
Business/es	Human Resources	Cleaning Services	Exporting
Husband: Partner	Yes	Yes	No
Hours Worked/Week	70	50	72
Household Help	Ft Nanny	Pt Housekeeper	Pt Family/Sitters
Years in Business	6	5	10
# of Employees	18	7	2
Report Gross Income	$85,000.00	$50,000.00	$1,000,000.00

My field research reveals that mothers are not prevented from working more than thirty-five hours per week simply by their maternal status. The resources in the household, including the ability to pay for help or call on relatives for support, condition whether or not the mother must be a full time care giver as well as a full time business person. Of course, a small number of women in New Jersey cannot represent a definitive pattern for entrepreneurs who are mothers of school age children. How men and women work and trade condition processes of cultural adaptation for people from different social backgrounds. But researchers who study the effects of work on family structure also find that women are able to manage their household responsibilities while working full time. Arlie Hochschild has described the dilemmas created for family's seeking cultural adjustment to women's full time employment in the United States (Hochschild, 1989). A recent longitudinal panel study by Karyn Loscocco and Kevin Leicht (1993) revealed that white women entrepreneurs are successful in balancing work and family demands. The domestic responsibilities of women entrepreneurs in Indiana do not account for gender differences in earnings between men and women.[4]

The spatial boundaries of women's lives in the suburbs have changed along with their roles as wives, mothers, consumers and family members. In New Jersey, the suburbs often surround an old town center. Single family housing developments cover what were once a patchwork of farms organized in townships. All three of the working mothers described in the chart above began their independent enterprises in the space of their homes. Mother One began her business at the kitchen table, making calls and putting together deals. But the demands of the business quickly outgrew the domestic space, and the business moved to an office building. Mother Two also began her business at home, but her neighbors complained about commercial traffic and activity on a quiet residential street. This forced the business out of the garage and into commercial office space. Mother Three works in the solarium of a large home, nestled in an exclusive, wealthy beach side community. Faxes pour into the solarium all day, which is organized with the latest slim equipment. Thus, a million dollar business operates in a space smaller than a suburban den. From the mobile work site of the automobile or cell phone to the kitchen table as a flexible work space, women's roles have adapted to the demands of independent enterprise. The middle class kitchen is more likely to be associated with deal making or coordinating household members' work schedules than with full time, domestic housewifery.

The marital characteristics of the research group, drawn from the middle classes in New Jersey, differs from those reported by the Department of Commerce in the *1987 Characteristics of Business Owners*. In the national survey, 70% of women owners were married, 9.5% never married, 12% divorced or separated, 6% were widowed, and 2% did not report their marital status.[5] Among the thirty-five women in the interview portion of this study, 54% are married, 20% are divorced, 23% are single and never married, and 3% are widowed. The New Jersey Association of Women Business Owners may attract more single and divorced women seeking support and a resource base outside the traditional family. As I note in the study description, the educational attainment of the women I interviewed was much higher than the national data used by the Department of Commerce; 60% held four year college degrees in the small, association-based group, compared to 18% in the national census of women business owners.

FAMILY AS A RESOURCE BASE

Marriage and the family are traditional resources, pooling material and emotional benefits for members. An important part of family support for women in New Jersey was the availability of informal loans, co-signed bank loans, and mortgaged family property as sources of capital. Families are important sources of capital resources, but we do not know if males and females will be treated equally with regard to informal loans by relatives. As I have noted before, the National Foundation for Women Business Owners

(1993) found that most small businesses, whether owned by a man or a woman, are started with less than $10,000.⁶ The primary sources of small capital funding for both men and women starting businesses are commercial bank loans and loans from family members. But bank loans are more difficult to obtain for micro capital in such small sums. Without collateral, the three women quoted below relied upon small amounts of family capital because they could not find a bank loan to finance small scale enterprise:

> I actually received $5000 and that's what I started this company with. $5000 and another $5000 from my husband's aunt. It was savings. It was bank loans. It was family loans. It was selling stuff off. It was everything. We just put everything into it until we had nothing left but the business.

> I borrowed the money from my parents but I'm going to finish paying them back this year. ....I got a leasing company to finance. I really didn't have any savings. ...Its like taking a loan out but its not a bank (dollar buy back or lease to own).

> I tried the small business administration, which I found to be totally useless and self-fulfilling in that they spent, as far as I'm concerned, their time sending out paper work so they could prove that they were doing something. Individual people were helpful. But basically, when they got to the next level they said sorry, can't help you. If you don't have assets, we can't loan you money. If you don't have a profitable business, we can't loan you money. I wanted to borrow $50,000. If you don't want to borrow a quarter of a million dollars or more, we can't help you. So I just got frustrated. And I found it was a lot easier to talk my grandmother into loaning me money.

This young woman depended on her parents for financial support. Her family floated a second mortgage to finance her business:

> My parents were incredibly supportive, obviously. They put the house on the line for this with all the money that they took out for me. But as things went along, they started to get a little nervous because I was not doing very well in my first few months. And I did have other relatives who said to my parents - don't loan her any more money. Stop now. Take your losses where you are. Sell the equipment, whatever. This isn't going to work. So I had a few relatives who did not think I was going to make it. But I did.

In a two-income household, the husband's salary provides a one to two year period in which this woman built her business.

> I love real estate advertising; that's my specialty. And I had this $300,000 account! And a contract! And meanwhile I'm running around interview-

ing and looking for jobs, and my husband said, "You're in business." I said, "No, I'm just free-lancing." He said, "Why don't you say you're in business and give it 6 months." I said, "I need a weekly paycheck!" I was panicked. He said, "You know, we're not gonna starve." The best thing about being a married woman entrepreneur, as opposed to being a single woman on your own not living at home, or a man with a family to support, is while we needed my income, we weren't gonna die if we didn't have it for a while.

I was scared. No question of that. I was very scared because it was a big undertaking. We take a chunk of our savings and I wasn't sure how it was going to turn out, but it's a gamble.

Despite her husband's income, the advertiser quoted above understood that the risk of capital in a small enterprise was her responsibility. Bankers often advise potential business owners to take a loan or mortgage against their house, which is one of the largest investments middle class families have. Every new entrepreneur works with the full knowledge that failure means going back to work for someone else with increased debts to pay.

EMOTIONAL SUPPORT AS A NECESSITY

Household forms and practices reflect the norms of the social environment in which women live and interact with others. Patterns of custom and belief in the society about motherhood have traditionally been part of an external normative order which coerces individuals to behave and think in terms of their care giving roles, whether they have young children or not, as the woman below describes:

I come from an era where women didn't work. ... I was a substitute teacher. And I was living in the town I grew up in. My family was there. And I did not win mother of the year award. I left my children and went to work. Even though it was teaching and I was home after school, my kids were little, I had a baby sitter, someone who loved my children. So they were in school full time.... it was tough, but by that time, women were starting to work. When I first went to work, women only went to work because they were starving—you know, poor people worked. Middle class women didn't work, especially Jewish JAPS. I mean nice Jewish girls grew up, got married—they weren't supposed to go to work. So I didn't win any awards from my family.

Women have balanced the necessity of work with customary sex-role expectations. Middle class women in the United States expect to define an individual identity in the working world through career and personal development.

The married women in this study strongly emphasize the importance of supportive husbands who believe in their choices. Spouses and domestic partners provide love, encouragement, and faith in the business owner's ability. Four women narrate their lives:

> Well, my children have been off to college. I've had grown children since I'm so mature, and that's been a good thing because it's given me more time for my business. And it's very hard. It's very hard to balance that time. Since it's just my husband and I and he's very supportive, we eat out when I'm tired. But you know, I have a very busy life. I manage to run a business; I manage to run a household; and yet socially we do a lot of things.

> When I give a talk to women who are thinking about going into business, I always say, "If you're married and you want to go into business and succeed, if you don't have a husband and children who support you, you have two choices: either get divorced or don't do it.

> My husband, as you've gathered, is very supportive. I'd say he's created the monster that I am, and he's always pushed. And he gets a lot of satisfaction out of my success. I often wonder what would happen if I was more successful than him, if he'd still be as happy, and I've got a feeling he wouldn't. But that's between you, me, the tape recorder and the world, not him.

> Well, marriage never came in the picture. We never worried about that kind of thing. Although I used to want to be married when I was twenty-three. But forget that now. I guess what it comes down to is - my parents were very supportive. They were pretty sure I could do it. Because they knew me, they saw me grow through college.....So my parents could see that it could work.....There was nothing like -I was married and I got a divorce and I had to, you know. There was nothing that happened. I think the biggest reason was I really just wanted my own thing. And I did not want to go back to school.... And I just wanted to do it. It just came naturally. Everything just flowed the way it flowed.

> The other people trained me to be driven and then my husband really pushed me to just go do it, you know what I mean. Who knows, maybe I would have been still farting around working for somebody else or doing something else. But he...Pushed me to really just do it.

The women business owners in this study do not report conflict between their family roles and business roles. They perform multiple roles, juggling difficult commitments that both allow them to maintain supportive relationships, and face traditional gender role expectations.

The family of origin may provide a source of models for small business ownership (Butler, 1991; Greene and Johnson, 1995).[7] Socialization in an entrepreneurial family firm included the acceptance of uncertainty and hard work which comes with small business ownership. Whether or not a daughter or niece is expected to inherit a family business, relatives with entrepreneurial experience can influence the choices of women, although they may not determine them.

> When I was in college, which was really when I first started in business. I had jobs prior to that but this is when I started learning about negotiating and deals, etc. Worked for the family business. But I was basically carte blanche. I did everything from buying, selling, putting together $100,000 deals and things like that. Because I could. Now my father was the boss. So he let me. ...I worked in a business which was dominated by men from all over the country. . . . and I worked for my father. So it was X's daughter. So it took me a while to be taken seriously because I was young. I was nineteen years old and I was someone's daughter.... then after a while people realized that I could handle myself in business.

The woman quoted in the following passage points out that out that the effects of environmental influences are cumulative rather than discrete. Family background is only one of the variables that shaped her choices in life.

> No, my family was always... very entrepreneurial—my father ... always had little businesses as I was growing up, a luncheonette, that kind of thing, and I just liked the idea of having my own business. Plus the fact that I had been a career person before I had my children, and then I stayed home those years and I like the idea of making my own decisions. I'm very independent that way. I like making my own decisions, and I'm able to make those decisions without dwelling on the regrettable part of it.

Although scholars often seek role models in the environment to explain entrepreneurial practice and behavior, the dominant teacher of strategies for organizing life does not have to be only one person close to the entrepreneur (Bygrave, 1994). We should not assume that the environment is consistent or that the dimensions of one part ("the family") determine the dimensions of another part (business) without active human choices. The socializing experiences of adulthood rather than childhood, which include learning to organize resources and solve problems in the work place, are the key experiences for the women in this study.

ACCESS TO CHILDREN AND THE NEW FAMILY BUSINESS

Both social scientists and popular commentators have speculated that women hope to find "flexibility" in their schedules to cope with the demands of motherhood and family life. Flexibility is a rationale to explain the choice to open a business. As this home-based publisher describes:

> (Due to pregnancy) My goals had to be realigned; changed my whole plan of action. That's when I decided to work out of the house.

The concept of flexibility presupposes that separate structures for work and personal life exist as organizing principles for everyday life, the home and the world, the office and the living room. It implies that work can be scheduled in blocks of time to give the working person more freedom to engage in separate activities, such as caring for young children. Caring for children and managing personal lives are often cited as a rationale for the risk of starting a business, but it is not easy to manage family and personal life when one is managing and growing a full time business. A mother of two children under the age of five, rejects the idea that business ownership is a solution to the demands of other role commitments.

> ...what scares me is I hear a lot of people saying - oh, I went into business because I have more free time for myself and I can make my choices and I can do that. I would say to you that's absolutely false. When you own a business you don't make your own choices, okay. You don't. Your market dictates to you what you're going to be doing. You can't just take off and go some place because you need to go there. You have to be there for your business. So I kind of reject that philosophy that a lot of people run around touting that - oh, I go into business and it's really satisfying because I can make my own hours and I can do this and that. I don't find that true for me. What I find satisfying is growing a business and making it real and being responsible for changing peoples lives.

These quotations from two women who are raising children illuminate the difficulty of balancing child care and business demands:

> It is difficult to raise children at the same time and really dedicate 200% of yourself to career.... one of the ways you can do it, is to start your own business. People used to say you can own your own business, because you can set your own hours and have that flex time. There is no flex time and what you find, and I've talked to a lot of other women, is that if you are willing to make it, you would end up working seven days a week, 12 hours a day. The convenient thing about this is I have access to my children and they have access to me. I am still able to come in here and do work and get things done.

I was a single parent. So having 3 children, I thought that if I had my own business at that time that I would have some flexible time or make my own hours. I would be able to take time off if I needed it, which I was totally wrong.

Fixed schedules help mothers to organize their household responsibilities, but it is difficult to manage a small business with a fixed schedule. "Access" is not identical to "flexibility". "Access" reflects the time continuum in which entrepreneurs work and parent young children. Parents must fit their children into the demands of their production and management schedules. There are no separate blocks of time. Flexibility is too often misconstrued to mean choices over how to accomplish activities in discreet and separate parts of life. "Access" flexibility involves discontinuous times that are secondary to the demands of making the business.

Instead of "flexibility," some women domesticate their businesses by employing their mates and kin. Traditionally small businesses owned by men have relied on the paid and unpaid labor of wives and children. One study that examines women in charge is Nicole Woolsey Biggart's *Charismatic Capitalism: Direct Selling Organizations in America* (1990).[8] Direct selling organizations such as Mary Kaye, the cosmetics firm, in which women are the main part of the workforce, require entrepreneurial behavior from the sellers in their network. Biggart found that the family was co-opted for use by the direct sales person as an extension of her business. Children and spouses became part of the organization. Women exploited their family relationships for the purposes of control and production in direct selling. Reciprocally, they strengthened traditional family ties while using the labor of family members for the business's purposes.

Women owners frequently bring their husbands and older teen age children into the work place as employees or partners, but no one described these relationships in purely instrumental or exploitative terms. This young gallery owner describes an intimate companionate marriage in which the organization of business time and personal time are fused:

I have experience in business and he doesn't. So we're completely opposite and completely compliment each other. And I've learned a lot from him about the creative aspect and he's learned a lot from me about the business aspect. But there's still definitely areas in which each of us are strong. He hates the telephone. He hates to make sales calls. I love to make sales calls. He doesn't like negotiating, I like negotiating. But certain things like writing scripts, we both like to do. So we work on that together.

Unlike direct selling organizations, I found that the structural organization of small businesses owned by women does not dictate the use and adaptation of family labor. Family partners and employees are highly valued and the salaries and compensation they receive strengthen their household security and kinship ties. Employment of kin represents a reciprocal distributive relationship that secures property and status in the family and reinforces the leadership of the owner or the partner couple.

When women make their husbands and children their silent partners, the business is interpreted as a "family" enterprise, and the gender of the founder is not highlighted. The old definition of a family business assumes women's subordination; the new definition of a family business reflects women's participation in the organization of family authority, property and credit. Women can amass independent investments, property and social leverage among their familial kin, while still maintaining independent public identities. In terms of gender relations, the power in a family business founded by a woman reflects distributive reciprocity rather than the direct domination by one partner, which characterized the traditional patriarchal firm.

CARE GIVERS, SUBCONTRACTING DOMESTIC LABOR

Behind middle class mothers' commitments to business is the labor of other women, house cleaners, babysitters and housekeepers. The exchange relationship between the dominant male bread winner and the subordinate female housewife has undergone a further division of labor in which the wife as an independent salary earner subcontracts the service labor for house work and child care to other women with less means, who may work for several individual clients. Women owners are continuously looking for labor to meet domestic and parental responsibilities. Household labor may be divided between more than one service contractor, for example a babysitter and a weekly house cleaner. Until other resources can be purchased, or if paid care provisions are inadequate, family networks provide child care. The following two woman relied upon supportive relatives and paid helpers:

> He's very supportive and helpful. [Her husband changed his work schedule to 3-11pm so he can watch their son while his wife works]. I've just hired a mother's helper. She's the second one I've had. She's a student.., but they're all unreliable so I can't really rely on them to set up meetings or appointments.....between (husband) and the mother's helper I have a lot of support.

> Yes, I couldn't have done it. My mother is here when I travel abroad, she stays with my children. I've had housekeepers that will stay. My sister helped me initially, she would take my children for awhile.

Instead of limiting their business activities around the demands of the family, many women discovered that they could organize their family lives around the demands of the business. As the economic support of her single-headed household, this narrative reveals that the mother's business was the first priority. How priorities are arranged can indicate the presence or absence of a partner or husband, whose support make a wider range of choices possible:

> I guess my priority has been the business and so they have kind of adjusted their schedules around it. I have set things up; not just the business with the office to be here, but their whole life style. Like where they're going to school. I don't have the time to play taxi mom, ... I make sure I am in an area where everything is convenient, either busing or bicycling.

Whatever the household form, I found practical, ambitious small scale organizers and managers who saw the family as a source of management problems and successes. A mother relates child care responsibilities to managing a business:

> Maybe that's why they've managed and done well, because they've had other things to manage. You know they say real life applications. You learn how to do it all and maybe that helps you with businesses as far as ups and downs and irate customers, and disappointments because it is all a part of life. And I guess when you have kids you go through that even more. And of course if you go through marriages that's another lesson.

Lack of child care in the United States is a structural barrier or a severe personal tax, placed upon any working woman who has to pay for help or child care. A working class woman who became a small manufacturer (forty employees), expresses the classic dilemma of mothers in the United States:

> It's difficult to be a working mother, if you own a business or not. If you value yourself as a mother, as the first teacher of your children and want to set them in the right direction.... this country is not built and does not provide the proper setting for women to go to work. Even if they are well educated or if they are a professional. There is almost no good solution for children. Knowing that was not what I wanted for my children I stayed home to raise them to a certain age. And when I found somebody to stay with them, that's the time I started going out to work as a part timer and then a full timer.

She sympathizes with the women who work in the factory because she was in their position when she started.

> They have to work....They have to work to support the family. And when you have to pay privately for someone to watch your child, that's a big chunk out of your salary. Especially if your income is low to middle.

Yes, there is definitely a lot of stress involved in trying to do that (raise young children). I had no choice, there are a lot of them out there that really don't have a choice. But it can be done. ....it takes a good woman to take on your children's part as well.... the preferred way to do it would be to establish a business before you have children or wait until the children are much older. So you can dedicate all that time and not have the conflicts or the kids home sick or the teachers calling you. Then that could go for any woman in a career. Where she's at a place of employment and have her children there and its the primary caretaker....

Individual families tailored solutions to their child care problems by patching together the resources and commitments the household could afford. Babysitters rarely make long term commitments, while family members may only be available within the parameters of their own schedules. Women still believe that the primary responsibility for child care is their own, but women entrepreneurs continue to search for practical support solutions.

SOCIAL LIVES, PERSONAL AND LEISURE TIME

Women business owners did not report feeling alienation from their loved ones because of the limited time available for leisure and family activities. They scheduled time with their children, spouses and companions, making their dates with them important breaks in their relentless calendar. The partners and children in their lives were often on their own schedules which also limited the time for shared activities. The distinction between the business calendar and the personal calendar was weak and often the two were fused. In the following passages two women report that the fusing of time frames did not create unmanageable conflicts in family life:

I try to spend a few days maybe an evening going shopping with the boys. Or taking them or going to an event that they have. They are all active in sports. So my social event for one week might be going to a basketball game, or going to a track meet. And that's part of being with them. And then I have clients that come in and then I have to entertain them. I guess that's a social activity, which is part of the business. Everything is kind of all wrapped up. I had a client come in from Saudi and he had to meet several manufacturers so I went to New York and then took him to meet this manufacturer, we had dinner with him and do that kind of thing. Or I'll take a client to a show. Take him down to Atlantic City or do something.

Rather than resenting a tightly scheduled life, entrepreneurial families in New Jersey structure activities and organize their playtime. There is "down time" or free leisure for entrepreneurial families, but it follows finished contracts. For some young couples as well as individuals, business swallows up their entire lives, encompassing both their personal and professional energies. But most of the women who I interviewed tried to take at least one day a week to spend in personal relationships.

Women business owners tend to be married to men who are active in business and social life. In New Jersey social activities with spouses include voluntary associations, arts and entertainment, and dining with friends. For example, this woman scheduled one to two nights of every week for 'doing something' with her husband.

> We're very active socially. I'm on the board of the Middlesex Chamber. I go to a lot of functions through the Chamber.... we have a subscription to the opera. We have a subscription to the George Street (regional theater). We're very busy. We're just busy people and we like that.

In the world of the small business owner, too much unstructured time would be suspect. Small business ownership is not a path to freedom from the constraints of conventional time schedules. Whether the self-employment path is a scattered cloud of events or a conventional girdle of 9 to 5, the proliferation of day planners and time keepers show human attempts to keep control over discontinuous events and shifting environmental settings. When a couple respects each partner's schedule and negotiates some personal time, self discipline and organization make choices more effective.

Women business owners do not want to be defined solely in terms of traditional roles and statuses attached to women's reproductive and sexual lives. These entrepreneurs have created their lives anew outside the middle class idea of 'home'. Women are willing to sacrifice social and business obligations when their children are sick, but otherwise they rely on a combination of relatives, spouses and hired help for the child care and daily housework that has so often been cited as a reason for their career limitations. Work and household demands are scheduled into a continuous calendar that allows access to children and leisure, but not the flexible freedom dreamed of by so many women. Apart from ideological assumptions about family and household forms, individual histories exhibit a diversity of strategies to meet the demands of personal life and business ownership. The women I interviewed successfully adapted female gender roles to the demands of employment and self-employment, breaking down both symbolic and real boundaries in the construction of their own lives.

CHAPTER NOTES

1. Cynthia Fuchs Epstein, *Deceptive Distinctions: Sex, Gender and the Social Order* (New Haven: Yale University Press, 1988); Arlie Hochschild, *The Second Shift* (University of California Press, 1989); Judith Lorber, *Paradoxes of Gender* (New Haven: Yale University Press, 1994).

2. Faye J. Crosby (ed.) *Spouse, Parent, Worker: On Gender and Multiple Roles* (New Haven: Yale University Press, 1987); Faye J. Crosby, *Juggling: The Unexpected Advantages of Balancing Career and Home For Women and Their Families* (New York: The Free Press, 1991, 1993); Rose Coser, *In Defense of Modernity: Role Complexity and Individual Autonomy*, Palo Alto: Stanford University Press, 1991; Cynthia Fuchs Epstein, "Multiple Demands and Multiple Roles: The Conditions of Successful Management," Pp. 23-35 in F. J. Crosby, (ed.) *Spouse, Parent, Worker: On Gender and Multiple Roles* (New Haven: Yale University Press, 1987).

3. The ages of each mother's children were averaged; these averages were then summed and divided by the number reporting.

4. Karyn Loscocco and Kevin T. Leicht, "Gender, Work-Family Linkages, and Economic Success Among Small Business Owners," *Journal of Marriage and the Family* 55 (November 1993): 875-887.

5. U.S. Department of Commerce, *Characteristics of Business Owners: 1987 Economic Censuses* (Washington, D.C.: U.S. Government Printing Office, April, 1992), Table 4d. P. 20.

6. National Foundation for Women Business Owners, *Financing the Business: A Report of Financial Issues from the 1992 Biennial Membership Survey of Women Business Owners*, October, 1993.

7. John Sibley Butler, *Entrepreneurship and Self-Help Among Black Americans* (Albany, NY: State University of New York Press, 1991); Patricia Greene and Margaret Johnson, "Social Learning and Middleman Minority Theory: Explanations for Self-Employed Women," (Draft) Department of Management, Rutgers University, 1995.

8. Nicole Woolsey Biggart, *Charismatic Capitalism: Direct Selling Organizations in America* (Chicago: The University of Chicago Press, 1989).

Political Issues and the Outlook of Small Business Owners

Apart from the organized efforts of the National Association of Women Business Owners and other associations and interest groups seeking to represent the self-employed, we still do not know if women owners will pursue a distinct politics, for example by widening the gender gap between political parties, or closing it. A study by Clarence Lo (1990) found that small business owners have been decisive participants in the tax reform movements in California and New Jersey.[1] This suggests that a political base may be built around specific issues of interest to small owners. The political issues the women business owners in New Jersey talk about in their interviews and everyday conversations reveal the economic and social pressures they must negotiate. Their commitments to family, local ties and self-interest, support an issue-based agenda that reflects both social and economic resources as well as constraints.

The election of Bill Clinton as President of the United States in 1992 brought debates about health care insurance and taxation by the state and federal governments into the forefront of middle-class dialogue in the New Jersey suburbs. Clinton's proposals for national change competed with those of Democratic Governor Jim Florio, who sought to increase payroll taxes for the support of public health insurance pools. Although small employers were being squeezed by rising health care costs, they opposed a tax on all employers to pay for a public health care fund during the Florio Administration in 1992. The NJAWBO leadership debated the health care agenda, a focus which emerged in the interviews. NJAWBO leaders also maintained a strong interest in privatization and wage laws, because of the small business owners' pursuit of new entrepreneurial opportunities and a sufficient labor pool. In response to open-ended questions about politics and what the state could do for women owners in 1992 and 1993, the women interviewed in this study focussed on these contemporary debates. Answers to an open ended question cannot completely account for a coherent "entrepreneurial politics," but the interview narratives indicate issues that were of concern to the women in NJAWBO.

The owners of small businesses are usually covered under the same health policies that cover their employees. They have a strong feeling of shared vulnerability.

> How could I not give myself health insurance? If I'm going to give myself health insurance, I must give it to my employees. That's the law, and.....I would love to be able to do the right thing, the strong moral thing.....I would love to have a dental plan. I would love to have my eyes covered. It's just not practical, the cost . . .

> I offer health insurance and a benefit package. And unfortunately I'm going to have to change and go to a lesser policy. But now I have problems. Because I have two children who are a little bit sickly. And I'm being told now - I'm going through some problems now because I'm being told that we can't switch because it'll hurt the employees. So now I'm faced with increasing their contribution rates, really. And it's going to hurt them. So I don't really know what I'm doing with my insurance now. Kind of in a quandary.

When asked about the rise in premiums for a private health insurance plan, a young woman with two employees exclaimed:

> Unbelievable. Unbelievable. Its horrendous, and we won't go to an HMO, because we, my partner and I, want to be able to choose where we go, you know, so that's something that can get me angry at a moments notice, that somebody's got to pay the bill, and it seems to be business. And I know that individuals feel the same way (that they've got to pay the bills and do not get enough help), but I'm also an individual.

> It's not so much the dollars and cents. If we were making $50 million a year and I could pay them anything I wanted to—I'm not cheap in that sense. I'm not greedy in that sense. I would love to have a top scale benefits program because I believe that they're necessary although I happen to believe that the price for insurance is absolutely insane.

The women in this study desire to offer their employees more secure and comprehensive benefits, but they believe they cannot afford to pay higher premiums for private insurance. The superiority of group comprehensive medical, dental and retirement benefits is clear and evident, but small employers claim they are constrained by private costs. Small employers feel too poor to pay for the system, although they long for the security of modern, collective solutions to social needs. The owner of a cleaning service discusses the moral dilemma of being trapped by the high cost of coverage:

> ...almost all of the business owners I talk to... They want to offer good benefits. They want to give their employees complete health care and stuff, but the sheer economics of it and kind of the way competition is structured in the market makes it very difficult for them to really carry the whole ball.

Women owners often feel powerless to change the larger institutional relationships in the society.

Federal and state investment in public health care funds could make small employers more competitive in attracting good workers, and remove the excess burden of diminished or expensive health insurance in the event of illness or injury drawing on the policy. However, the concept of the universal system mediated by a central government, 'federalizing' the health care benefits system, is met with skepticism even by people who recognize the need for reform.

> Because it's just a Band-Aid (payroll taxes and employer contributions). That's not what the problem is. The problem is the abuses in the system. The things that have gone wrong for the last umpteen years. That's what the real problem is.

Instead of increasing the small business owner's support for a centralized, public system, the inefficiency and expense of health care is attributed to unfair politics and systemic problems in the structure of the industry.

Distrust of the government is common, particularly at the federal level, because it is viewed as coercive and self-serving, or it appears to organize reforms in the interest of more powerful groups. A personnel service owner expressed this cynical belief that the government and other organized interests have disenfranchised her in the health care debate.

> I have to admit that I'm not even listening to what is happening in the health care issues, because I know I will have no influence. I don't have a clue as to what the answer is. I wouldn't know how to contribute even if I did. I personally believe that government is self-serving. I think that they've lost track of the fact that they're here to serve us, and this idea of a health plan is definitely necessary, but I don't know who its going to serve. Anybody's plan, I really don't know who the "Benefactors" are going to be.

While the insurance companies must compete for the independent business owner's dollar, the state and federal governments redistribute tax revenues to many constituencies. Distrust of political solutions is compounded by the expense of the private system in which coverage for married employees is often redundant, taxing each partner's employer.

> Do you offer your employees health insurance?
> Yeah, we do. We pay for it, but I have to say for the most part our people are already covered in other plans, either their spouse's plan or the plan under which they retired, and they can get a better deal than what we can offer.

By hiring women who are married or retired, small business owners are more likely to find employees with preexisting coverage who do not object to lower benefit levels.

Business owners understand that the economy is structured through multiple, often fragmented, levels of institutional policies, contracts and relationships. In the quotation below, an owner establishes that the relationships between the small employers, federal government, unions, which are market-based interest organizations, and employees, reflexively structure the economy of New Jersey.

> Well what's happened is the unions are blaming business and small businesses that they don't care about employees and they don't provide health insurance ... and they don't really care. .... So they want to put a 2_ percent payroll tax on employers payroll to pay for this uncompensated care fund. Which is going to run out and actually has run out and may be extended. And what will happen is, it'll devastate New Jersey. Because small businesses can't afford to pay for health insurance for their employees. There's no way. It's too expensive. My health insurance costs just went up and I can't afford a plan. I've had to switch from a very good plan to a cheaper plan.

Large corporations, small businesses and governments, may have competing definitions of a good outcome for policy; these definitions must be compromised in order to work with the other participant groups in the political framework.

> We were talking the other day about the initiative and referendum bill. For big business, it's a positive. For small business, it's not. It's like for big business they have the dollars and the lobby and they can get things done through the INR where small business doesn't have that kind of clout, so you have major differences in perspective. The other thing is like the health care, the new health care payment they're trying to pass, the health care tax, where if you don't offer health care, you have to pay a payroll tax. There's a big difference between the large corporations who are already offering all these benefits and who don't want to pay an extra payroll tax because they're already offering all that and the small business

that can't afford to offer those kinds of health care packages. There's a big difference between the two perspectives.

A source of tension and contradiction in the structure of business and the business community's attitudes toward political issues occurs between large corporate capital and local small business. Large corporations have different needs, and a wider scale and scope, while small businesses are interdependent with large corporations in the health of regional and local economies. Small business owners want stability in the local economy and low operating costs. Service business owners want relationships with large corporate clients. They aspire to achieve large corporate status, the size and success to "go public," and their subordinate interdependency with larger businesses is desirable. The small owners in NJAWBO expressed a 'live and let live' attitude toward big business.

> The interests should be the same. Big business I don't think concerns itself too much with small business in terms of looking at them as any kind of competition or looking at them in a threat in any way although this country is, the economy of this country is largely small, what the government classifies as small business. And that's the bulk of where our economy is generated. I am not really one in favor of a very strong government interference or government regulations at all.

Large businesses can influence the government by threatening to move to other cities, regions or countries. To stave off "capital flight", local, state, and national governments compete to attract and keep large businesses because these organizations provide employment and tax revenues which redistribute economic benefits throughout the economy. In a "capital strike" corporations stop investing in expansion and maintenance, hastening the decline of a business facility. The threat of capital flight or lay offs by small employers is less compelling than the threats made by large employers. Small employers want to keep large corporations in their state and in their local region, because their economic activity generates demands for small business products and services, either through the spending of their employees or subcontracting.

But to the owner embedded in the local scene, government appears to be dominated by large interests. This perception reinforces the strong individualist ideology of these two small employers, who complain:

> The states themselves? I think they're trying. I think part of the problem is that any bureaucracy is difficult to get things accomplished. ...obviously they've got other agendas. But that's just me. But I realize that what's good for me is not necessarily good for everybody.

...there's not enough programs for small businesses. Small businesses feel left out. They don't know how to get involved. That's why I said the partnership with big business is very, very important. Because we all want to stay in New Jersey and we all want to create good businesses. And big business depends on small business to be their vendors. And they've gotta be there. And if they're not there what's going to happen to the big business? They're going to go too.

Defensive political postures sometimes lead business owners to reject the legitimacy of political processes and government authority. The two women quoted below do not trust government authority:

All I know is I have to comply with so many rules and regulations, reportings, and it boggles the mind. Its so hard to keep up. They claim they're simplifying it (the paperwork), I don't think they're supportive at all, and I think by the nature of the fact that they are a government; they're so far removed from what we have to do, they don't have a clue.

How would you describe your politics in your own words?
My politics. I think as I learn more about making videos and understanding that what you show people is often what they believe. I kind of think we don't know anything about politics. We have no idea what politicians are doing, what they say, what the media tells us they're doing. It has nothing to do with what's really happening.

One activist, chair of the sub committee on health care for the Middlesex County Regional Chamber, who opposes government initiatives, said:

I just want to do business in a healthy state and let the state be healthy and let the economy work by itself. Stop the government from poking its nose into the businesses. Businesses are competitive. The competition will drive you out....Now I'm not saying that we shouldn't have government in just anything. But stop that feeling of entitlement . . . Oh, I deserve more programs. But where's the money going to come from? It's going to come from me.

Professional lobbies are extensions of those organized interest groups that small holders find suspicious, as the woman below attests.

I'm not a very big believer in lobbying. It's so much money. I mean I guess if you were to classify the way I think about a lot of things, I come out of the fifties more than the sixties or seventies. I am very conservative. I think that people should get what they deserve, good or bad. I think that you earn what you get. I don't particularly care for situations like we're describing. It boils my blood.

California small property owners formed an organized movement to resist the power of federal and state governments which divert resources away from the small property owners' immediate community control (Lo, 1995). The women business owners interviewed for this study expressed a strong preference for the personal ties they developed at the levels of state and local government, in voluntary associations and in the Chambers of Commerce, in contrast to general legal obligations to the public good imposed by a federal authority.

The national association parent has a political agenda that is communicated to all members through publications and political education materials. For example, NAWBO supports federal and state subsidy of public education and training, calling the transformation of America's schools "our number one priority." Their approach to human needs includes privatizing social services and 100 percent tax deductibility of health care premiums for employers. In the following quote from the "2020" report, the economic interests of small business classes are emphasized in terms of converting privatized social services into franchising opportunities:

> Franchise opportunities are now cropping up in industries ranging from preschool education to domestic and commercial cleaning services, and from computer sales and servicing to construction contracting.
>
> Governments are utilizing franchising as a means to privatize previously government-owned services, such as the postal service in Brazil. Through franchising, it is possible to break up large government entities into small-business opportunities, rather than merely selling a large publicly-owned firm to a large private corporation.

When it comes to competition for the potential contracts on which privatization will rest, NAWBO wants a franchising system rather than open bidding, thus asserting the interests of the entrepreneurial classes as democratic levelers in the face of the superior power of large corporations. By couching their claims in terms of what is good for America as we approach the 21st century, NAWBO fights for entrepreneurial class interests by steering carefully through many potential conflicts in the entrepreneurs' relationship with workers, government and large corporations, avoiding issues of downsizing, lower wages and benefits, less secure pensions and new limits on public service that follow privatization of public services.

In an attempt to bridge local and general interests, a publication of the National Association of Women Business Owners presents community development as an opportunity for entrepreneurs to be leaders.

....the problems of America's communities must be solved within the human heart—by a commitment to individual responsibility; the desire of change for the better; and the leveraging of community resources by gifted leaders who can impart vision, empower and inspire people, and give them the courage to take action to realize their shared dreams. America's can-do entrepreneurs—who can overcome all obstacles and dream great dreams— are the ultimate community leaders who will revitalize our communities.[2]

The pursuit of a local base for political power and leadership does not exclude alliances, compromises and deal making with other class and social interest groups in the society. At the grassroots level of suburban town, county or district, locally based business owners have the greatest opportunity to control the use of resources. The entrepreneur below expresses a desire to control a greater share of federal revenue through locally controlled programs:

I don't think the federal government has really done much other than pay lip service to a lot of things. I think that the funding that we've received from the federal government for the Excel program is a major, major breakthrough in this country and could really lead to a lot of very positive things for a lot of women in business. If we can contain that kind of thing, funneling money into the private sector to provide educational training for women owned businesses then I see that as the best thing that the federal government can do, take the money out of their own hands and put it out so that people can use it.

Women owners want the government to help them subsidize their costs, just as any business class seeks to provide for its interests. The entrepreneur below recognizes that social policies subsidizing the cost of training and education are beneficial to small employers:

Would you like to see the government and the state providing more capital funds?

More capital funds mostly for training. And to help us get better employees. To give the employees what they deserve and without taxing us and burdening us we would like health insurance and things like that. I think that is very important.

From your perspective would a national health insurance plan take pressure off of your employees?

It will take pressure off of employees and it would probably provide us with better employees. It would give freedom to some employees to move from job to job instead at a certain job if they had health insurance.

Small employers in the contemporary United States report that they do not perceive themselves to be part of an organized interest group which can change the government, while those owners who do organize politically, often do not feel that they are able to exercise sufficient leverage in the political system to realize their collective interests (Lo, 1990). Studies of small shopkeepers in the United Kingdom have found that they are Conservatives "by default", because they are against big government and anti-union (Bechhofer and Elliott, 1978; Aldrich, Zimmer, Jones, 1986).[3] To quote a home based publisher:

> I tend to support the Republicans; I really have no party affiliation. I tend to go with whose doing what and what's better for my business.

Small business owners are not trained economists, and very few of them have an education in economic theory. Rather than a studied strategy based on a shared sense of political participation, free market ideology has become part of the everyday repertoire with which ordinary people resist taxation and regulation by the state and federal governments. For example, the owner of a nonunion cleaning firm in Middlesex County who pays her workers seven dollars an hour, reports that her bids to enter a building under a union contract were unsuccessful. She considers the regulations that maintain the union wage structure, which guarantees more than ten to eighteen dollars an hour to be unfair restraints on free market trade.

> we had a chance to get about $80,000 worth of carpet cleaning on a quarterly basis.... All the carpets were gonna be done 4 times a year.... It was about 35% of what they were paying. Our fees were really, really low. They would have saved about $120,000 a visit. We couldn't do it.... It was in New York, a union building.
> So there's a lot of things that happen in this country that are not in my opinion legal (kosher). It's legal to do that, by the way. You can have a closed building and only allow union members in. Some of the other things that I think are absolutely ludicrous; the government has certain clauses in there that say that you must pay living wages, or customary wages. And it costs the government probably a couple billion dollars a year for that cost. What it means is that if I come in to a government contract that I have to pay my employees the prevailing rate in that particular location for unionized help. And I have to pay unionized benefits.
> (So that could double the cost of your labor?)
> No, it could probably triple it.

People who do not see the necessity of these competitive forces are believed to be trying to limit entrepreneurial opportunities. Most firms owned by women are in business services which depend on stable clients.

Ideological beliefs in the free market hide the degree to which small business owners are limited by their own fierce competition. There is nothing to stop the cleaning business down the block from trying to undercut the bid of the woman from Middlesex County. Their niches are subordinate to the needs of larger firms which try to cut costs at the expense of service suppliers. Unrestrained competition may be bad for both small firms owners and employees, because it holds down both profits and wages. Low incomes restrain the purchase of healthcare and retirement accounts, and keep small owners running in place at the bottom of their industries.

While small business owners tend to oppose increased government regulation and taxation, there are diverse reasons to form political interest groups. A young gallery owner objected to my characterization of NJAW-BO members as conservatives by asserting her pro-choice beliefs about abortion and her skepticism about organized politics:

> I have a real problem with the label like that [conservative] because I think part of it is I have issues that cross over. I would say, just on a gut reaction I supported the democrats kind of feeling an inclusion versus the republicans. ...I don't really label myself. I certainly have strong ideas about particular issues. Pro-choice.

> I think I don't mind high interest rates because now the interest rates are low but nobody can get any money. And I know people like my grandmother was on a fixed income and was getting 15 percent on her CDS and now is getting 4 percent. So I would like to see the interest rates go up, more money available. I don't necessarily have a problem with government involvement and things like international trade to prevent the Japanese from restrictive trade agreements and things like that. More money available for businesses. And I think that things like requiring students to put in a year of work is a real good idea. More community involvement. Tax credits... I know that when it was easier to get money, it was easier to make money. Even if you have to pay high interest for it.

Political affiliation, identity and action are mediated by a complex interplay between ideas and issues that must be confronted in part outside the framework established by associations and political parties. Businesswomen report that their relationship to the state and the federal governments is uncertain and ambivalent, but their search for common interests does not preclude political strategy or the need for social policy.

CHAPTER NOTES

1. Clarence Y. H. Lo, *Small Property Versus Big Government: Social Origins of the Property Tax Revolt* (Los Angeles, CA: University of California Press, 1990), pp. 133-138.

2. National Association of Women Business Owners, *2020 Vision: Entrepreneurial Policies for the 21st Century*, (June 11, 1995), p. 8.

3. Howard Aldrich, Catherine Zimmer and Trevor Jones, "Small Business Still Speaks with the Same Voice: A Replication of the 'Voice of Small Business and the Politics of Survival'" *Sociological Review* 34 (May 1986): 335-356; Frank Bechhofer and Brian Elliot, *The Petite Bourgeoisie: Comparative Studies of the Uneasy Stratum* (New York: St. Martin's Press, 1978).

Federal Policy and the Market Solution

From the early 1970's onward, small business legislation and policy reflect attempts to forge an empirical consensus of support for increasing the distribution of federal resources to aid small businesses. Along with new aid and advocacy programs, the United States Federal government has sought to resolve or balance the disadvantaged position of ethnic and racial minorities, women and all small businesses in relation to large corporations, government regulatory agencies and labor markets. In the course of small business activism in the 1990's, the legitimacy of government as an institution balancing individual and collective interests has been tied to the legitimacy of the market solution, the belief that capitalist free enterprise will create successful strategies for the resolution of social inequalities. Based on the market solution ideology, legislation designed to help women achieve greater equity in the small business world does not address the patterns or processes of structural inequality that reinforce women's subordinate status.

SEARCHING FOR PROTECTION AND EQUAL ACCESS

The 1970's were characterized by women gaining access to better jobs and independent consumer credit. At the same time they continued to be subject to explicit discrimination. Women were still asked for a male relative's co-signature on credit applications. Marital status was a criterion of credit worthiness. First enacted by Congress in 1974, the Equal Credit Opportunity Act (ECOA) was designed to end discrimination based on marital status, and to open access to consumer credit regardless of sex. It also required lenders to keep a record of applications and to inform applicants of the reasons for denial of loans. In 1976 Congress amended ECOA to prohibit discrimination based on race, color, religion, national origin, age, public assistance status, or applicants' exercise of their rights under consumer credit protection laws.[1] Women provided an expanding consumer market for credit cards and contributed to long term growth in the use of credit cards for the purchase of goods and services.

The federal regulation for the implementation of the ECOA, Regulation B, (12 C.F.R. section 202 (e)), distinguished between consumer and business credit in ways that maintained the status quo of sex discrimination against women in commercial lending. It exempted business lenders from the prohibition against inquiring about marital status, and relieved them of the responsibility for record keeping and notification of reasons for rejection. In 1978 the Federal Reserve Board withdrew a proposed rule change that would eliminate Regulation B, with the rationale that the close relationship between creditors and business applicants made the marital status question inconsequential.[2] The National Organization for Women argued that sexism was shaping interpretations of women's suitability for business management and entrepreneurship, but federal regulators did not respond to their complaints. Organized women's groups were not strong enough to counter the claims of the banking industry that the ECOA rules were costly and unnecessary burdens that should not be expanded. Like other civil rights protections, law suits under ECOA were difficult to win. Women had gained the general right to buy on credit, but as sellers in market relationships, they were dependent on commercial credit obtained through personal relationships with male bankers. Women had not yet achieved protection from discrimination.

During the 1970's attempts were made to protect small businesses from the unfair competitive advantages of large corporations. A pattern of tiering regulations according to the size of business developed, effectively exempting small business from many new reporting and compliance rules. Small chemical companies were exempted from testing and reporting requirements mandated by the Toxic Substances Control Act of 1976. The Occupational Health and Safety Administration curtailed reporting regulations for firms with less than twenty employees. Businesses with fewer than fifty employees were exempted from filing affirmative action plans with the Office of Federal Contract Compliance. Small business associations argued that the cost of regulation outweighed its social utility. Small business alliances and opposition to regulation by central government attained greater legitimacy with each following decade of legislative change.

Women business owners were in the contradictory position of calling on government to create stronger protections against discrimination in the openness of credit, capital and trade, while they participated in small business associations such as the Chambers of Commerce, which opposed government regulation of business relationships. Women in business associations supported a liberal social agenda, in which government should protect the rights of women as full citizens, and a conservative or laissez faire economic agenda, in which interference in market processes was defined as undesirable.

The Regulatory Flexibility Act (RFA) of 1980 created tiers of regulation according to the size of the firm. Congress found that uniform application of federal regulatory requirements cost small business' money and time, and created barriers to their ability to effectively compete. The RFA attempted to protect small business class interests against the domination of both large businesses and federal power. It failed to meet the goals and ambitions for more autonomous control by small business owners in the 1980s, because government agencies did not have to account for the costs regulations imposed on different sizes and kinds of business organization; there was no official proof that a particular regulation was the cause of hardship for small business.

Despite the legacy of tiering, workers in small businesses are still covered under federal wage and hours, civil rights and anti-discrimination laws, although it is difficult and expensive for them to pursue court cases against employers. Part of an owner's local reputation is based on how well they treat "their people," and this social evaluation influences their ability to attract and retain good employees. Local customs and regional differences in the history and use of labor may condition how people assess and judge a small business owner's practices. Business and trade licensing and industry self-regulation through trade association guidelines are also ways in which small businesses conform to good practices. Licensing may be required at local, state and federal levels, providing a series of checks for health, safety and product or service quality.

Small business owners are constrained by federal, state and local laws not specifically targeted to them. For example in 1992, one topic of conversation in the New Jersey Association of Women Business Owners was a new state law requiring property owners to pay for the clean up and removal of abandoned oil storage tanks on their property. While not explicitly directed toward small business, many small property owners were forced to look at the environmental history of their sites in order to comply. Today commercial property in New Jersey is rarely bought or sold without an environmental survey, creating a business for small firms that conduct the research. In short, tiering did not free small business owners from labor, health, safety and environmental regulation. Compliance with government regulation remains a disputed "burden" or social necessity, depending on the small business owner's political perspective.

THE 1980'S AND PRESIDENT REAGAN

The 1980's were a boom time in the expansion of the service economy and consumer credit. The greatest contributions to favorable conditions for small business owners during the administrations of President Ronald Reagan (1980-1984-1988) were first, an economic boom in service industries financed by credit, and second, popularization of ideas that market processes were far superior to government policy as sources of strategy for both economic and moral regulation. The ideological promise of the "free market" in which profits trickle down and market demands trickle up to the producers, was a powerful basis for political action, because it promised to create a massive redistribution of wealth to capitalists. According to neoclassical economic theory, capitalists large and small should raise wages, hire more workers, and meet the challenge of a greater number of entrepreneurial competitors.

During the 1970's and 1980's there was considerable investment in manufacturing plants overseas. The ideological argument that increased free market competition would impose discipline on the American working class, diverted political attention away from the structural dilemmas of responding to the international shift in capital investment.

David Birch, the MIT economist, generated a politically charged debate about small businesss employment as a market solution to economic growth in *Job Creation in America : How Our Smallest Companies Put the Most People to Work* (1987). Birch argued that the small business economy was generating most of the new jobs created in the 1970's and 1980's. This position became popular with political conservatives who believed that government regulation of capitalism was unnecessary because market processes would produce economic growth. President Reagan voiced strong support for creating the market conditions from which moral and economic regenerations were supposed to spring through entrepreneurship.

As the number of small service firms in the United States expanded, the political importance of small business owners as interest based, diverse voting constituencies increased. The rapid expansion in the service sectors of the United States doubled the number of small business owners in the economy. The number of women owners also doubled during this time. The rapid growth in women's business ownership in the new entrepreneurial economy built a potentially influential base of political support among a small number of women capitalists in their states and localities.[3] This insured that political attention was paid to women's representation when the role of small employers was discussed or debated.

One example of the emerging contradictions between official ideology and the new entrepreneurial class politics centered on the role of the Small Business Administration. President Reagan tried to abolish the SBA out of the belief that it represented overregulation of the economy, a waste of government money that was not necessary in a free market economy.[4] While the Reagan administration considered rapid growth to be proof that government intervention through a separate agency was unnecessary, the SBA was a resource for the growing number of self-employed, who fiercely defended its necessity and legitimacy against the President's plan to downsize the bureaucracy. Bowing to pressure from the large Republican constituency among small business owners, he backed away from his attacks on the SBA. As a popular conciliatory move, President Reagan hosted a White House Conference on Small Business in 1986 for 1,813 delegates from around the country to make recommendations for Congressional action. The delegates were elected from small business forums in each state. White House Conferences are called as a representative forum in which small business owners directly communicate their concerns to the President and the Congress, distinguishing their economic and social goals from the concerns of other organized interests. The 1986 meeting was a tribute to the social importance of the entrepreneurs, but it did not result in significant legislative change. White House Conference recommendations live or die based on sufficient political support in the Congress.

The National Association of Women Business Owners made the contradictory argument that bias limited commercial lending to women, but concurrently, that women's inexperience was at the root of their disadvantage in market exchange processes. Education and counseling were at the forefront of the NAWBO policy recommendations to increase women's entrepreneurship in the 1980's. These ideas reflected a Conservative agenda that downplayed the ongoing force of sexist prejudice. If women were participating without social restraints in free market processes, then their lack of progress in expanding their businesses and hiring more workers could be attributed to their own inexperience. The Women's Business Ownership Act of 1988 (HR 5050) appropriated $10 million dollars to the SBA over a three year period to develop long-term entrepreneurial training and counseling programs around the country. Like other loan programs administered by the Small Business Administration and local loan ventures, the provision of this money was largely symbolic. Few small business owners receive SBA loan monies, but the programs providing them are well advertised. The women I interviewed in New Jersey referred to federal money as "band aids," "more symbolic than real," and "frustrating to apply for." Yet government does gain some favor by directing money to the SBA.

The faith of entrepreneurs in pure, laissez faire market processes during the Reagan and Bush years, ended after the economic downturn of 1989. Education was not the real barrier to women's access to capital, but the political focus on education did not challenge the popular belief in the free market as a source of social discipline and value. By the mid-1990's many women possessed at least a decade of managerial experience. Among small business owners in general, women sought more strategic, interest-based protections from government.

A STRONGER HAND IN THE 1990'S

In the 1990's the federal government responded to the needs of small businesses by seeking to protect them from large corporate monopolies, promoting social policies to strengthen the interdependency between businesses at all levels, and enhancing the service role of the Small Business

Administration. Improved government reports were devised to include regular corporations as well as small businesses, and to distinguish self-employed individuals from small firms, thus increasing the visibility of small employers as a group deserving government consideration. Women business owners became more prominent public actors, symbolically integrated into larger plans to coordinate changes in the economy, while struggling to gain a better deal in business relations.

The social construction of gender differences in business settings have further complicated the role of the government in defining a small business agenda. Inequalities between men and women in access to capital, credit and trading opportunities have been addressed by political initiatives, but these inequalities are not resolved. During the administration of President Bush, women were recognized as a group which deserved strengthened federal protection. The Federal Deposit Insurance Corporation Act of 1991 (FDICIA) amended the ECOA (1976) to require bank regulators to report directly to the Attorney General any pattern or practice of discrimination or discouragement by a banking institution.[5]

Another issue complicating claims to redress gender inequities in access to capital resources is the size of entrepreneurial firms and the relative importance of such firms in the domestic economy. Small firms have never achieved full equality with large corporations in their relationships with large banking institutions. Investment banks in the late nineteenth century United States expanded to provide capital for the growth of large corporations, not the struggling middle classes of small family firms and farms (Chandler, 1990), whose children and grandchildren joined the new classes of twentieth century white collar workers (Mills, 1953).[6] The scale and scope of businesses have been a basis for divisions in political interests throughout the history of industrial capitalism. For example, in the 1840's in Britain, the state protected the interests of large property owners against the claims of other classes and interest groups in capitalist society. The landed aristocracy were the rivals and often the enemies of the nouveau riche manufacturers in fierce political struggles for control of parliamentary legislation.[7] Large businesses usually have more assets than small employers to leverage as collateral when they apply for credit or loans. Today, the size of a commercial loan is still a consideration in the approval process.

The new entrepreneurial middle classes in the late twentieth century have defended their relationship to large corporate capital, but they have also pressured the federal government to balance their capital needs through the Small Business Administration and to redress unfair economic conditions that may result in corporate monopolies. Citing the merger of BankAmerica and Security Pacific in 1992 as "anti-competitive for small business," the Justice Department required the divestiture of 211 branches in five Western states to prevent market domination by one corporate banking organization.[8] The Justice Department raised an objection to a corporate merger, because it determined that the merger would cause the price of small business services to rise by five percent or more. While faced with unfair advantages of scale and scope which create corporate market domination, the small business owners' political alliance with large corporations as part of the business sector lobby may not be easy to maintain.

President Bill Clinton's proposals in his first administration (1992-1996), including the formation of a national health insurance program, mandatory employer provided benefits, and the North American Free Trade Agreement, were opposed by small business associations, although national health insurance pools would have greatly reduced the burden on self-employed individuals and small employers who cannot afford Health Maintenance Organization (HMO) coverage. Nonetheless, President Clinton was responsive to pressure from small businesses for the control and limitation of government agency regulation. In 1993, Clinton strengthened the RFA of 1980 in Executive Order 12866, which required federal agencies to look for alternatives to regulation, to design regulations in the most cost-effective manner, to design regulations to impose the least burden on businesses of different sizes, and to take into account the costs to business of cumulative regulations.

The Congress strengthened the power of businesses in relation to government regulators and lending institutions by creating new entitlements and rights for small business classes. The Small Business Regulatory Enforcement Act of 1996 transformed the RFA into a defensive arsenal for small businesses to resist new federal regulation and compliance with existing regulation. Regulatory agencies are required to publish agendas, hold forums and solicit opinions from small business owners about the impact of regulation, send new regulations to business owners, create small business advocacy review panels for each rule that may have an economic impact on business, and compile regulatory flexibility analyses to weigh the economic impact of changes. The law also allows the Chief Counsel for Advocacy with the SBA to intervene as an amicus in court proceedings involving compliance with the RFA, and gives a small business owner the right to seek review of a rule's compliance with RFA in court. Reversing the trend toward federal regulation, small business owners have recently gained more political power and the promise of relief from government supervision.

THE ENABLING STATE AND THE BACKBONE OF THE NATION

According to Neil Gilbert at the University of California, the new entrepreneurial economy is an important structural basis for theories of "the enabling state," or the transformation of the welfare state through policies which increase privatization and market based solutions for the provision of employment, human needs and services to people who are poor or challenged (Gilbert, 1996). In the political climate of the last fifteen years, the Congress put forward policy changes which emphasized community control, privatization, and the devolution of welfare protections into work programs and market solutions to the human service needs of the poor.

The "Republican Revolt of 1994," led by Newt Gingrich in the House of Representatives, offered a new Conservative agenda for the Congress that favored small business interests. The *New York Times* reported that 60 percent of the Republican freshman grew up in small businesses, and believed that the "business-government partnership" excluded them.[9] The Republican-dominated Congress set in motion structural changes in American society, redefining or abolishing social welfare entitlements for the poor. In mid September of 1995, eighty-seven out of one hundred senators voted to dismantle the welfare state, resulting in the passage of the Welfare Reform Act of 1996. The Personal Responsibility and Work Opportunity Reconciliation Act of 1996 (PRWORA), signed by President Clinton on August 22, 1996, requires public assistance recipients in good health to work, and imposes time limits on the receipt of assistance.

These changes have particular relevance for women workers and women entrepreneurs. Over ninety percent of welfare parents are women with one or two children, who are likely to be employed in small to medium entrepreneurial firms.[10] Women living in cities, suburbs and rural areas will experience different opportunities for participating in the entrepreneurial expansion of the economy because the location of industries and patterns of ethnic and socio-economic residence are not uniform in their relationship. For example, the rural poor will have few chances of finding work in fast food or business service industries, while the urban poor will need clear English speaking skills to work in most service jobs being created by the current expansion in the economy. In some localities service sector expansion is weak or non-existent, stranding those citizens who cannot imitate the more affluent urban and suburban middle classes. Women entrepreneurs tend to be concentrated in more heavily populated urban and suburban states such as California and New York, where they are competing with larger, labor-hungry corporations for low wage workers.

The Welfare to Work Partnership is a not-for-profit organization formed by an alliance between government and private capital to facilitate the employment of welfare and workfare recipients across the country. The Partnership was formed by President William Clinton, and Governors Tommy Thompson (R-WI) and Tom Carver (D-De), on May 20, 1997 at The White House. The goal of the Partnership, including the federal government, United Airlines, United Parcel Service, Burger King, Monsanto, Sprint, and over 100 participating businesses, is to "hire individuals from public assistance without displacing current workers."[11] According to The Partnership, there are four million people who are potential wage earners among the eleven million recipients of public assistance.

Since the formation of the Partnership, Vice President Albert Gore has become active in soliciting support among voluntary association networks which can further facilitate the training, education and employment of welfare recipients in their localities.[12] Beside the Chambers of Commerce, this includes club-based associations such as the Rotarians and The Elks, which attract both executives and small business owners. The new role of voluntary associations in providing placement, advice and other intermediary services for the Welfare to Work Partnership, also strengthens these organizations in political and moral, as well as economic, importance in American culture. Under the Clinton-Gore Administration, Ronald Reagan's dream of entrepreneurial leadership as a source of economic growth and social discipline is about to be tested. The motives behind the new enabling policies may be symbolic, because they appease and attract business constituencies which are useful for political parties to win elections. But symbolism reinforces the belief that entrepreneurial capitalism can be a source of order and discipline, thus influencing how people perceive their choices and the options of other people.

THE MARKET SOLUTION: RHETORIC OR RESOLVE TO CHANGE?

The Small Business Act of 1997 (PL 85-536, as amended) highlights the federal government's new role in the protection and promotion of small business classes in the United States. First, by encouraging the market competition of businesses, the federal government proposes to resolve the disadvantaged position of racial and ethnic minorities, women, and small business in relation to government and big business. This degree of resolution is impossible to achieve with a single act of legislation, but much can be learned from how the language of the bill describes the social structure of American society in terms of market ideology.

Small business is defined as the mainstay of national security because of its role in the "free" enterprise system:

> Sec. 2. (a) The essence of the American economic system of private enterprise is free competition. Only through full and free competition can free markets, free entry into business, and opportunities for the expression and growth of personal initiative and individual judgment be assured. The preservation and expansion of such competition is basic not only to the economic well-being but to the security of this Nation. Such security and well-being cannot be realized unless the actual and potential capacity of small business is encouraged and developed.

To accomplish greater national security and well being, the redistribution of federal monies to small business programs is increased. Small businesses, rather than military force or corporate capital, are symbolically positioned as backbone of the Nation. Middle class nationalism is equated with universal security. An imagined community (Anderson, 1991) of small capitalists in competition will regenerate the economy and society. But the ideological faith in such a class transformation of social structure may be difficult to achieve in reality.

The Small Business Act includes many parts that are explicitly written to further women's participation in business, including capital and business development programs.

> (h) (1) With respect to the programs and activities authorized by this Act, the Congress finds that—
> (A) women owned business has become a major contributor to the American economy by providing goods and services, revenues, and jobs;
> (B) over the past two decades there have been substantial gains in the social and economic status of women as they have sought economic equality and independence;
> despite such progress, women, as a group, are subjected to discrimination in entrepreneurial endeavors due to their gender;
> (D) such discrimination takes many overt and subtle forms adversely impacting the ability to raise or secure capital, to acquire managerial talents, and to capture market opportunities;
> (E) it is in the national interest to expeditiously remove discriminatory barriers to the creation and development of small business concerns owned and controlled by women;
> (F) the removal of such barriers is essential to provide a fair opportunity for full participation in the free enterprise system by women and to further increase the economic vitality of the Nation.

The attempt to remove discriminatory barriers emphasizes the legitimacy of the federal government in the redress of inequitable access to capital and credit among different classes of people. Women are officially recognized as a group facing special challenges, who are essential to the vitality of the Nation. But the loan monies provided for women and minority small business owners are the only detailed remedy for inequality, and the application for such monies will favor individuals who are already familiar with business practices.

As welfare is restructured, federal revenue is earmarked for more small business loans to women, minorities and to businesses in areas with high unemployment. Section 2 (d)(1) stipulates:

> The assistance programs authorized by this Act are to be utilized to assist in the establishment, preservation, and strengthening of small business concerns and improve the managerial skills employed in such enterprises, with special attention to small business concerns (1) located in urban or rural areas with high proportions of unemployed or low-income individuals; or (2) owned by low-income individuals; and to mobilize for these objectives private as well as public managerial skills and resources.

By encouraging the investment of small businesses owned by women and minorities, the government structures a market solution to unemployment and the relief of poverty. Stronger alliances between employers large and small, along with the voluntary sector, are a primary goal of the new policies. Class situation is ultimately market situation (Weber, 1978).[13] Under this new law, the internal stratification of entrepreneurial business classes, as well as the multi-cultural diversity of groups in the United States, are not adequately addressed. The true beneficiaries of these legislative changes may be regional business alliances of owners with stronger market positions.

Women entrepreneurs and their allies have strengthened the federal government's commitment to the equal protection of women and minorities in business relationships with banks and creditors. As small business owners gained in political importance, their representatives' attacks on government regulation and oversight increased, along with demands for a greater share of redistribution of funds to small business in the form of loan programs or strengthening small business services and advocacy. Women are recognized as a status group which has suffered from discrimination in business relations, and therefore women, along with African American and Hispanic minorities, are collectively eligible to apply for loans earmarked for their use by the Small Business Association.

The market solution to inequality is a political approach to managing the contradictions in women's relationship to employment in the entrepreneurial economy. Poor women will have to find ways to live under the new conditions that will be generated by the devolution of the welfare state, through participating in entrepreneurial schemes to commodify care giving responsibilities for children, and "fitting" into the low wage service economy. It places the burden for emerging from poverty on the individual. New loan monies for small business formation and expansion will not resolve systemic inequalities rooted in patterns of race and gender difference, but they will benefit women entrepreneurs who are able to capitalize on opportunities created by the economic expansion in the 1990's and the new political leverage of small business. In any scenario, the pro-entrepreneurial policies will require new levels of both public and private investment in the social and economic integration and growth of small firms in the United States, and a politics emphasizing small firm owners' rights in relationship to the larger polity.

CHAPTER NOTES

1. In states with common law property statutes, wherein property acquired during the marriage was assumed to be under the management and control of the husband, or under joint control, women's marital status continued to be relevant in credit assessments. The joint property exemption placed women under special review, but had little effect on married males. U.S. Department of Commerce. *Women and Business Ownership: An Annotated Bibliography*, (Washington, D.C.: U.S. Government Printing Office, 1986).

2. U.S. Department of Commerce, *Women and Business Ownership: An Annotated Bibliography* (Washington, D.C.: U.S. Government Printing Office, 1986), p. 66.

3. U.S. Department of Commerce, *Women and Business Ownership: An Annotated Bibliography* (Washington, D.C.: U.S. Government Printing Office, 1986), p. 3.

4. Mansel G. Blackford, *A History of Small Business in America* (New York: Twayne, 1991), p. 109.

5. Fried, Frank, Harris, Shriver & Jacobson. (1995) "Fair Lending Time line." [Online]. Available: http//www.ffhsj.com/fairlend/timetest.htm [1998, January 26].

6. Alfred Chandler, *Scale and Scope: The Dynamics of Industrial Capitalism* (Cambridge, MA: Harvard University Press, 1990, 1994). Also see C. Wright Mills, *White Collar*, (New York: Oxford University Press, 1953).

7. G. R. Searle, *Entrepreneurial Politics in Mid-Victorian Britain*, (New York: Oxford University Press, 1993), p. 2.

8. Michael Quint, "Shift in Scrutiny of Bank Mergers," *New York Times* (Monday, May 11, 1992), p. D7.

9. David E. Sanger, "Seismic Shift in the Parties Reflects View on Business," *The New York Times*, (Sunday, September 24, 1995), Section 4, p. 1.

10. The Urban Institute, Welfare to Work, http://wtw.doleta.gov/ohrw2w/recruit/urban.htm [July 23, 1998].

11. The Welfare to Work Partnership, [1997] http://www. welfaretowork.org [July 23, 1998].

12. Vice President Gore's Welfare to Work Coalition, Members of Vice President Gore's Welfare to Work Coalition, [1998] http://www1.whitehouse.gov /WH/EOP/OVP/Work/members.html [July 31, 1998].

13. Max Weber, *Economy and Society, Volume Two* (Berkeley: University of California Press), p. 928.

Conclusions Amid Changing Conditions

Individuals join a "women's association" such as the New Jersey Association of Women Business Owners because it functions in both public and personal ways that are beneficial to them. The association's programs subvert lingering cultural prejudices that limit women to subordinate roles in business. The National Association for Women Business Owners fights for the expansion of women's roles and women's rights as part of an ongoing struggle to change the limiting gender boundaries of social structure and cultural practices. Practical integration strategies strengthen women's cause and link women entrepreneurs to shared agendas. A woman's association works to overcome the cultural resistance of men and women who interpret women's roles as limited, and to strengthen individual self-identity so a woman continues to pursue her goals in the face of lingering sexism. Association encourages women to refer their identities to entrepreneurs and small business owners in general and teaches them methods to do so. Models of individual success function to legitimate women's risks of resources when they choose self-employment. The New Jersey Association of Women Business Owners thus creates a strategy for women's integration into market and society.

Suburban businesswomen have encountered different sources of uncertainty that create incentives for them to go into business, such as sexism, divorce, downsizing, corporate transfers, career barriers, unemployment, and limitations in the range of their work roles as employees. Yet, the refusal by association members to make gender the salient focus of every interaction, undermines the assumption that collective gender status is a causal force in women's behavior as entrepreneurs. They are motivated to escape from work regimes in which the conditions of control are supervised by levels of managerial authority above them. Although among my interviews forty-three percent are former executives, it is not necessary to hold an executive position to learn business practices. Non-supervisory white collar workers also learn how business is conducted, by carrying out many of the administrative and support functions that are necessary to make deals. Individual careers develop through interaction with people doing business, and by solving every day organizational, production and delivery problems.

Relative to salaried employees, successful self-employment gives the entrepreneur a position of freedom from conventional time schedules and close personal supervision, with the added dignity of self-definition in reference to more successful independent capitalists. Among the middle class with resources, ownership enhances an individual's opportunities to realize new selves because of the roles and relationships involved in sustaining an entrepreneurial identity, increasing work satisfaction. Women with material and social resources benefit from entrepreneurial opportunities by capitalizing on their knowledge, credit, savings and social connections.

Suburban women have transformed kitchens, dens and spare rooms into centers of production, adapting the spaces available to them. More successful individuals can afford offices in commercial buildings. The women who participated in this study preferred to have offices separate from their domestic spaces. But individuals do not limit their activities because of traditional proprieties about what a woman should or should not do in the parlor or the kitchen. They are focused on the practical uses of time and space to support their businesses. Motherhood is not a barrier to business ownership, and it may or may not be one of the reasons a woman pursues independent ownership. As owners, mothers achieve limited access to their children rather than total flexibility in their care giving schedules. Women do not report feeling deep conflicts between their professional and personal lives. Individuals have reorganized their household and family obligations around the demands of their careers. These changes in the organization of daily life depend on the creativity and adaptability of individual entrepreneurs. By overcoming impediments to communication, sharing information and clarifying the terms of trade, women and men are rationalizing gender roles by adapting their beliefs to include the integration and participation of women in business.

Women business owners in suburban New Jersey have achieved a new position in business, but it is difficult for them to overcome economic and social constraints. The majority of businesses owned by women are in service and retail niches of the local economy. The average individual income among women in the study was only $40,000. The incomes from small businesses do not place the majority of these working capitalists among the social elite. Faced with the competitive advantages of larger businesses, small firm owners must continuously market themselves and prove their trustworthiness. Women tend to form businesses in service and retail industries, a pattern which reflects the development of their knowledge in similar occupations. But individual women are pursuing a much greater range of business roles, challenging sex-typed limitations. Individuals must continue to break through the size and income barriers that place the majority of firms owned by women in the small scale margins of the economy.

Despite the widening opportunities for self-definition, middle class women's beliefs about gender differences continue to shape their self-interpretations and narratives. Some women define their businesses as "children" and "families" requiring close attention and supervision. But the demands of the management role structure the daily practice of business to a greater extent than beliefs about gender. Since most women own small service businesses, personal relationships between the owner and workers characterize the labor process. Operating with less than ten employees in local markets, close supervision and strong interdependency between the owner and workers develop on the shop floor. This may include many strategies, such as empowering employees to make independent decisions in the solutions of problems, defining employees as a second family, employing contract workers, part timers and leased employees, or simply duplicating the impersonal managerial strategies of corporate offices. Full time owners work long hours to meet contract demands. They need to secure labor and information they can trust, even when they only can afford to hire part time, casual or out-sourced workers. Hiring and seeking advice by word of mouth through associations or other social ties provide small business managers with more reliable references for their labor and management needs.

Women entrepreneurs are not a unified political interest group. As individuals, their political commitments are focused on identification with "community," the locality, region and personal relationships in which they live. This local orientation is common to small property owners who want government resources to be under local control, where people who share their business class concerns are more likely to hold power. Stresses from the costs of doing business, paying for health insurance and tax obligations, influence their opinions. Employers in small enterprises, like the people who work for them, are in need of collective solutions to social problems that government policies should address, such as the costs of health care, training, and retirement benefits, but they are skeptical about the efficacy of solutions they feel are not designed to meet their individual interests. Their beliefs in individual strategies in market processes as a path to prosperity become the basis for issue-based political activism.

In the struggle to overcome the legacies of sex discrimination and sex-typing, the members of the National Association of Women Business Owners and the National Foundation for Women Business Owners are trying to secure their best advantage by developing relationships with large corporations, the media industries, politicians and powerful interest groups. They are joined by many other men and women with the same goals, better opportunities for the women at all levels of business. These tactics have unintended consequences, reinforcing the pressure on individuals to find market solutions to their own disadvantage and diverting attention away from large scale structured inequalities. This diversion may not benefit all women.

In the future, women will continue to use their business experiences to start entrepreneurial firms. There are long term changes underway that create more open trading structures and new kinds of relationships. Today, millions of people do business on-line in virtual trading communities that reduce the need for face to face interactions. There should be fewer gender-related constraints. But the internet and its diverse worlds will not replace local markets or local business cultures as the basis for social integration in the structure of business. The ways people interact and communicate in their everyday communities support cultural patterns that are the basis for negotiation and cooperation in exchange relationships. Local cultures can conserve expectations about gender roles in business that place women at a disadvantage. Out of necessity, women have become increasingly articulate advocates for their own interests in business. The state and federal governments must continue to support equal rights and equal protections under the law as society and economy change over time. The legitimacy of market-oriented, entrepreneurial society will depend on adherence to the ideals of open negotiation. Overall, women who own entrepreneurial firms have won respect for their efforts and expertise. Despite daily struggles and confrontations with inequities, the business owners I spoke with remain optimistic about the benefits of managing their own margins.

APPENDIX 1: METHODOLOGICAL NOTES

The social establishment of a sociologist in the field involves a process similar to the one I describe in the life of a woman entrepreneur. First, through interaction with each participant in the study, I had to define my identity as a researcher and my affiliation with the City University of New York. Second, I had to establish myself in the women's business association, and distinguish my project from competing social scientists who were in contact with its membership. Third, in meetings of the American Sociological Association and the Eastern Sociological Society, I shared my ideas and delivered interim papers; thus, I established a place for my project among other professionals investigating similar subjects. My abilities to articulate my identity, my goals, and my professional affiliations were attributes rooted in cultural resources.

My first challenges as a field researcher was to find people who were willing to participate in open ended, face to face interviews. In 1992 I became a participant observer in the New Jersey Association of Women Business Owners, an organization of roughly one thousand members organized in thirteen county chapters divided in three geographical regions. The members of New Jersey Association of Women Business Owners do not share a unified geographic community, but they do share a common suburban culture. Over a two-year time period, I attended chapter meetings in north, central, and southern regions, including Union, Middlesex, and Northern Monmouth chapters. I also received the NJAWBO newsletter. New Jersey is ranked ninth in a list of states ranked by the proportion of businesses owned by women, and is among the top ten states with concentrations of all businesses.[1] New Jersey is situated between New York City and Philadelphia; both of these cities continuously host concentrations of women owned businesses that are among the top ten in the United States (US Census, 1987). The association is a strategic research site in a state which exhibits both national patterns of change and a significant concentration of the business owners who provide the evidence for these findings (Merton, 1987).

I combined several strategies of inquiry: (1) observation of the New Jersey Association of Women Business Owners local chapter meetings, (2) in-depth, focused interviews with thirty-five women who own independent businesses, (3) nineteen informant interviews, (4) historical analysis of social and economic structural change in the United States since 1970, (5) analysis of NJAWBO chapter newsletters and publications, (6) analysis of U.S. Department of Commerce reports derived from Census and IRS data, and (7) analysis of National Foundation for Women Business Owners reports and press releases. Informant interviews consisted of unstructured conversations over dinner or lunch, usually at public events such as meetings or conferences. I wrote notes based on these conversations. In addition, I interviewed the Chief Executive Officer of the American Women's

Economic Development Corporation and three members of this association's million dollar round table.

I collected my interviews in two ways: (1) At random, I called every fifth name in the Union and Middlesex chapters listed in the New Jersey Association of Women Business Owners Membership Directory (1991); this accounted for more than one third (14) of the depth interviews conducted. (2) During my participation in meetings and in conversations with small business owners, people often gave me the name and number of someone they knew who owned a business inside and outside of NJAWBO. Using this snowball technique, I made contacts for twenty-one (21) interviews. The use of a limited directory and snowball contact methods was not random, but the directory was a strategic research tool for entering networks to which I had no other access. The depth interviews were conducted at each owner's business; this allowed me to explore the terrain of each person's everyday workplace. The interviews ranged in time from forty minutes to more than two hours. I used an open-ended interview guide [Appendix 2]. The interviews were transcribed onto floppy disks by typists, and hard copies of the transcripts were printed. I analyzed the data by reading the transcripts and reviewing select audio tapes to discern themes for generalization. Quotations from 31 interviews appear in the text.

Participants in the study are owners of private firms who belong to or attend voluntary associations of women business owners, either the New Jersey Association of Women Business Owners or the American Women's Economic Development Corporation. All the businesses in this study employ less than fifty people, with a range of zero to forty employees. This is far below the 100 to 500-employee standard used by the government to categorize a business as small. Regardless of sex, most small businesses recorded by the United States Census reports are comprised of individuals who do not employ others, and report negligible incomes. I adopted a flexible rule of thumb for my study: the owners had to derive their primary income from the business (not including the household income contribution of spouses), work in the business at least 35 hours per week (full-time), or assume responsibility for the management and executive direction of at least half of its daily operations.

THE NATIONAL AVERAGE COMPARED TO THE STUDY

How well does the non-random sample of women owners who participated in this study fit the known characteristics of the national surveys of women owners included in the Department of Commerce data? I compare the characteristics of study participants with findings reported by the Department of Commerce in the *1987 Characteristics of Business Owners*.[2] This report is based on a survey of businesses taken from the Internal Revenue Service and economic census records. My sample data are based on a questionnaire given to thirty-five women who were interviewed in person. The women who participated in the study were asked to return the completed survey by mail. Sixteen questionnaires were returned. Each question had a different number of individuals reporting the requested information. In addition, some of the description data was culled from the depth interviews on tape or transcript. I tried to retrieve as much information as possible for descriptive purposes. The informant interviews conducted at dinner meetings and events were not structured sufficiently to include in the following comparison notes.

BUSINESS DISTRIBUTION AND INCOMES

Industry

Twenty-seven of the women I interviewed owned service businesses, two women owned financial service or planning firms, two owned retail stores, two women owned design and construction businesses, one woman owned an exporting business, and one woman was a manufacturer. This pattern reflects gender clustering and stratification in industries. In 1987 service industries accounted for 55% of women owned businesses, but only 22% percent of total receipts for women owned businesses. The next largest concentration was in retail trade, with 19% of firms and 31% of receipts.[3] A random survey of 8,000 small businesses in New Jersey, conducted by the Bank of New York in 1994, found that 54% were service businesses, and 24% were retail businesses.[4] Men start businesses in the same opportunity niches that women do, but women start few businesses where men have been predominant, high technology, manufacturing, engineering and skilled trade firms. These patterns reflect the clustering of gendered individuals, not absolute segregation.

Business Types

As noted above, most businesses are sole proprietorships, unincorporated small businesses. In this study, 46% of the business owners manage sole proprietorships, 37% manage corporations, and 17% have partnerships. This distribution is more evenly distributed than the national survey sample, in which 90% were sole proprietors, 4% percent were partnerships and 6% were subchapter S corporations.[5] In the "S" form of incorporation, the owner's income and business income are taxed as one sum. For example, if the corporation earned one hundred thousand dollars, that corporate income would also be the owner's income on a federal tax form. In a classic "C" corporation, the income of the business is taxed as a separate legal entity, apart from the individual incomes of owners and managers.

Years In Business

Women in my interviews report that they have, on average, six years invested in their present business. This indicates stability and experience among the members of the New Jersey Association of Women Business Owners. Among the sole proprietors in the national survey eighteen percent were in business five to nine years. The modal category of 24% was one year or less, two years equaled 15%, three to four years accounted for 13%. The numbers drop to 8% in business ten to fourteen years, 5% percent have fifteen to nineteen years, 3% have twenty to twenty-four years, and 4% have twenty-five or more years.[6] While the study average matches the largest percentage over one year in the national survey, the Department of Commerce figures include more new business owners and less well educated individuals who earn low incomes.

Income

Out of fifteen people reporting their individual incomes, the average income was $40,000. with a range of $6,000. to $100,000. This sample statistic fits the national data for household income, which indicates that women in NJAWBO are better off financially as individuals. The modal household income for women business owners in 1987 was $25,000 to $49,000. dollars, which accounted for 35% of the distribution. The bottom of the national survey was larger than the top; 23% of reported incomes were over $50,000., and 35% report incomes less than $24,999.[7] Women business owners are middle class, and the women in this study are not among the wealthiest elites in New Jersey.

Business Receipts

A statistic that is closely related to income is the gross receipts of the firm, from which the owner takes either a percentage or a fixed salary. The fifteen women who answered the income question do not match the fourteen women who reported their business gross receipts. The modal category of business gross receipts was $51,000. to $100,000, with five respondents checking this category. The average reported gross was $466,544.79, with a range of $20,000. to $2,000,000. Three women reported gross receipts of $101,000. to 500,000. One woman checked the $501,000. to 1,000,000 category. Three women reported gross receipts of more than one million dollars, and two women reported receipts of less than $50,000. Three women reported taking 15% to 20% of their business gross as a salary, but they refused to define their gross. Income and receipts indicate a middle class economic base among the sample.

Members of the New Jersey Association of Women Business Owners maintain cultural norms that safeguard individual privacy. Women invest labor, time, energy, and pride in their businesses. Asking an individual to name her income is like asking for the price of her wedding ring. Advertising one's income is not done, because it immediately intrudes class stratification into an association committed to the equal participation of all individuals in the market. More affluent women report their business gross receipts as a measure of their success. But some women may be reluctant to report modest middle class incomes. Small owners may be protecting their financial status as a safeguard against solicitation. I was asked more than once if I could assure participants that the information I collected would not be sold or used in consulting projects.

Hours

The average work week for the women interviewed consisted of 55 hours per week, with a range of 20 to 80 hours.[8] Due to a failure by the Department of Commerce to distinguish employer firms from all self-employed individuals in the calculation of average hours per week, it is difficult to compare the study with the national average. Only 11% of the national survey worked 50 to 59 hours per week; 5% work 60 to 69 hours; 4% work seventy or more hours per week. Assuming that a full time work week is at least 35 hours, it is surprising that only 8% work 30 to 39 hours; 9% work 40 hours; and 9% work 41 to 49 hours.[9] Overall, the number of hours reported was lower than I expected.

Employees

Only one quarter of all businesses in the United States employ anyone in addition to the owner. A business is categorized as small if it employs under 100 people (U.S. DOC., 1978). Less than one million of the four million women-owned businesses in the 1987 Census had paid employees. Three-quarters or 78% had fewer than five workers, but 13% employed five to nine; only 9% employed ten or more.[10] We can characterize the women in this study as micro-employers. The average number of employees for the 27 women owners responding to the question is six, with a range of one casual worker to 49 payroll employees. Twelve women in this sample, almost half, report employing three or fewer workers. The sample statistic average appears to be higher than the national average because of two outliers employing more than 45 people.

PERSONAL CHARACTERISTICS

Age

The average age of women in the study was forty-three years old, with a range of twenty-eight to sixty-five years. This matches the modal category of age for women owners in the United States. According to the U.S.

Department of Commerce, in 1987 only 3% were under age twenty-five; 19% were 25 to 34; 29% of women owners were thirty-five to forty-four years of age; 22% were forty-five to fifty-four years old; 16% were fifty-five to sixty-four; and 8% were over age sixty-five.[11] This age distribution reflects the prime working years in an adult's life. Women owners are not retirees seeking to supplement income; neither are they young women waiting to start careers or families.

Level Of Education

Study participants were highly educated. Sixty percent of the women interviewed had achieved Bachelors Degrees, 12% possessed Masters Degrees, 17% were high-school graduates, and 11% did not report their education. In contrast, the national survey included more high school graduates, 30%, while 8% did not graduate from high school, 21% had some college education, and 18% graduated from college. Sixteen percent possessed graduate degrees; 7% did not report their education.[12] My findings are strongly biased toward the views of educated, active women. Educated women may be more likely to seek the support of a business association.

Marital Status

Among the women interviewed there were more divorced and single women than the national survey. Fifty-four percent were married, 20% were divorced, 23% percent were single, and 3% were widowed. One of the divorced women and two of the single women privately admitted being lesbian, 9% of the sample. In the national sample 70% were married, 9% never married, 12% divorced or separated, 6% were widowed and 2% did not report their marital status.[13] The disparity in these percentages suggests that the New Jersey Association of Women Business Owners may attract single and divorced women seeking a support and resource base outside the traditional family. While married women need social support and information, the association also provides an outlet for finding friendships.

Religious Self-Affiliation

The modal religious self affiliation of the women in this sample was Protestant, but the distribution of affiliations was almost evenly distributed. The sample was 34% Protestant, 29% Catholic, 26% Jewish, 3% nondenominational Christian, and 9% reported no religious affiliation. There is no national comprehensive data with which to compare the study findings. I can only speculate that the majority of women business owners are Christians, mirroring the general population. The settlement patterns in suburban New Jersey included waves of upwardly mobile post-World War families from New York City, including large numbers of Catholics and Jews. This may account for the religious distribution in the sample.

Many ethnic and religious groups are not represented in this study. Within the national sample, 86% were born in the United States. In this study, 34 out of 35 women interviewed were native born. People of Buddhist, Muslim and Hindu faiths are recent immigrants to suburban New Jersey who tend to join ethnically based associations. The entire non-random set of interviews in the study included only two native born, African American women. The distribution of such a small number is simply descriptive of the findings of this project in predominantly white suburbs.

CHAPTER NOTES

1. National Foundation for Women Business Owners, *A Compendium of Statistics on Women Owned Businesses in the U.S.* (Silver Spring, MD: NFWBO, 1994), p. 27.

2. U.S. Department of Commerce, *Characteristics of Business Owners: 1987 Economic Censuses* (Washington, D.C.: U.S. Government Printing Office, April, 1992).

3. The statistics in this section are calculated from the 1987 *Census of Women Owned Businesses*, Table 1 and Table 10.

4. The Bank of New York (NJ), *2nd Annual Report on the State of Small Business in New Jersey* (October 1995), p. 4.

5. U.S. Department of Commerce, *Characteristics of Business Owners: 1987 Economic Censuses* (Washington, D.C.: U.S. Government Printing Office, April, 1992), Table 4d. p. 20.

6. U.S. Department of Commerce, *Characteristics of Business Owners: 1987 Economic Censuses* (Washington, D.C.: U.S. Government Printing Office, April, 1992), Table 14d. p. 96.

7. National Foundation for Women Business Owners, *A Compendium of National Statistics on Women-owned Businesses in the U.S.* (September, 1994), p. 3-5; U.S. Department of Commerce, *Characteristics of Business Owners: 1987 Economic Censuses* (Washington, D.C.: U.S. Government Printing Office, April, 1992).

8. The number of hours worked per week were often reported as an estimated range. If someone replied that she worked 60 to 80 hours a week, the lower number was used in the cumulative calculations for the sample average.

9. U.S. Department of Commerce, *Characteristics of Business Owners: 1987 Economic Censuses* (Washington, D.C.: U.S. Government Printing Office, April, 1992), pp. 66-67.

10. National Foundation for Women Business Owners, *A Compendium of National Statistics on Women-owned Businesses in the U.S.* (Silver Spring, MD: NFWBO, September, 1994), p. 2-3.

11. U.S. Department of Commerce, *Characteristics of Business Owners: 1987 Economic Censuses* (Washington, D.C.: U.S. Government Printing Office, April, 1992), Table 3, p. 12.

12. U.S. Department of Commerce, *Characteristics of Business Owners: 1987 Economic Censuses* (Washington, D.C.: U.S. Government Printing Office, April, 1992), Table 3, p. 12.

13. U.S. Department of Commerce, *Characteristics of Business Owners: 1987 Economic Censuses* (Washington, D.C.: U.S. Government Printing Office, April, 1992), Table 3, p. 12.

APPENDIX 2: INTERVIEW GUIDES AND QUESTIONNAIRE

GUIDE FOR FOCUSSED INTERVIEWS WITH BUSINESS OWNERS
Name: Age:

I. WORK HISTORY AND HISTORICAL PLACEMENT (Experience in time, and economic action in temporal perspective)

Describe your business and its history.
What year did you start and where were you located?
How many hours did you put in at first and how many do you put in now?
What was your work experience before you started your own business?
What led you to decide to start a business?
What was your vision of the kind of business this would be?
Is this a sole proprietorship, partnership, or corporation?
Were business conditions good when you started, or did you have real
    ups and downs?
What were/are your greatest problems?
Where did you get the money to start your business? (If more than one
    business: to start your first business? to start your current business?)
Did you apply for loans when you started? (from a bank? from the Small
    Business Administration?)
How would you describe the experience?

II. COGNITIVE ASPECTS (Construction of the self, active interpretation of identity and choices, through which individual places self in culture)

Can you think of any major changes in your life that influenced your
decision?
When you went into business, did you feel yourself changing? (Was this
sudden or gradual, how would you describe it?) If you had to describe
(Name Respondent) in three words, what would they be?

How did other people around you respond to your decision to go into
business? (Friends, co-workers, household?)

What is the most satisfying aspect of owning your own business?
What is the least satisfying aspect?

What did you expect when you started?
Have things turned out differently than you expected?
Where do you imagine yourself in ten years or twenty years? If you had it
to do all over again, would you still start your own business? (Index satisfaction)

III. CULTURAL ASPECTS (Collective understandings, patterns of belief, ideology and practice which shape economic actions and goals)

What is your educational background?
Are you married or do you have a partner? Who lives with you?
Have you ever been divorced?
What does your mate do for a living?
Does your mate work in your business?
Has your household changed since you've been self-employed?
How do you balance your time between personal life and business?

Do you have children? If so, What are their ages?
If a parent: How old were your children when you started your business?
How do you manage being a parent with your other responsibilities?

Do you feel that women and men face different obstacles in business in general? (Description?)

Is your style of doing business and managing based on some particular principles? (Opinion. Probe for ways of dealing with people and customers)

IV. SOCIAL ASPECTS (Patterns of social relations, networks of association, and the social construction of market relations)

Do you have employees? How many Full Time and Part Time?
How would you describe your relationship with the people who work for you?
How often do you deal with them on a daily basis? (Part-time? Temp? Full time?)

How do you hire? Do you put an ad in the paper, or go through word of mouth, or hire away people who you meet in the business?
What makes a good employee for your business?

Do your customers have a typical profile?
How did you find your first customers, or how did they find you?
Do you have a strategy to build your customer base?

How did other people help you to set up your business? Follow up, specify: family, friends, a consultant, organization like NAWBO, SBA, particular book, other?

Do you belong to any community and business organizations?
Have they helped your business?

Do you socialize with the people you do business with?
How about the people who work for you?

V. SOCIAL RELATIONS/FAMILY BACKGROUND

What is your ethnic background?
Where did you grow up?
What did your parents do for a living? What was their education?
How many brothers and sisters do you have? What do they do?

If from a business owner household: Did your parents help each other with the business?
How many hours a week do you think they put in?
Did you feel part of it, did you work with them, or was it their work?

Were there other business owners in your family? What kind of business were/are they in? Were you familiar with it? Did you ever work for them?

Who were you closest to in your family?
When you were growing up, did you ever imagine yourself at the head of your own business?

VI. POLITICAL ASPECTS (Position of women business owners in relation to power mediated through access to capital and credit, the law, the state, and the changing demand for labor and services)

Could you suggest any changes in the law that would help your business today?

Have you actively supported any lobbying efforts on behalf of small and independently owned businesses? (Probe for specific plans, policies, laws, proposals)

Do you see small businesses and big businesses as partners with complimentary interests, or do you think the interests of big business and small business are different?

Do you feel that the state of (New Jersey) is supportive of small businesses and entrepreneurs?
Do you feel that the federal government has helped or hindered people in your position?

How would you describe your politics, in your own words? Do you prefer a particular political party?

Do you feel that the demand for your business is secure in the present economy? How would you describe an ideal economic future for your business?

How much did you business gross last year? Do you give yourself a salary or do you take a percentage? (Dollar Amount?)

VII. NJAWBO SUPPLEMENTARY QUESTIONNAIRE/ MEMBERSHIP

1. How long have you belonged to the New Jersey Association of Women Business Owners? What year did you join?

2. From your perspective, what would you say are the most important activities of NJAWBO?

3. What are the best aspects of participating? Are there any drawbacks? (Competing with people in the same business?)

4. Have you ever served as an officer or on a committee?

5. What kind of activities and issues would you like to see NJAWBO take up in the future?

6. Do you see yourself as part of a national movement of women into independent business ownership, or more as an individual who made the choices that were open in her time and place?

I want to thank you for your time and participation in the study.

POST-INTERVIEW QUESTIONNAIRE

All replies to the following questions will be held in complete confidence and no information on this page will be directly attributed to individuals who appear in the text of the study. The following questions are for purposes of comparison only, to create a statistical profile of business owners who have responded. Thank You For Your Participation in This Study!

Age:　　　　　Male or Female:
Number of Years In Business?
CATEGORY OF BUSINESS AND YEAR FOUNDED:

INDUSTRY:
Current Business Type: Sole Proprietorship, Partnership, Corporation? Other?
Number of Employees, Full Time/Part Time:
Gross Receipts Last Year:
Your Gross Net Income From Business Last Year:
How many other businesses have you owned or do you currently own?
Number of Hours You Personally Put In Per Week?
Circle Appropriate: Married, Single, Single-Divorced, Widowed, Life Partner
What does your mate do for a living?
If Applicable, Is This Your First Marriage?
Age at First Marriage?　　　　Age at Second Marriage?
Age at Divorce?
Number of Children in Your Household:
Ages of Your Children:
People Who Live In Your Household (SPOUSE, PARTNER, CHILDREN, OTHER FAMILY MEMBERS):
Percent of Total Household Income You Bring In: 0-10%, 11-30%,
　　31-50%, 51-70%, 71-100%
Do Mate or Other Household or Family Members Work in Your Business?
If yes, how many hours a week do they put in?
Total Household Income in 1991:
　　a) $10,000. to 50,000.; (b) $51,000. to 99,999.;
　　c) $100,000. to 499,999. (d) $500,000. to 999,999.;
　　e) $1,000,000. to 4,999,999. (f) $5,000,000. plus.
Ethnic Background:
Your Religion:
Primary Residence: Urban, Suburban, Small Town, Rural

BIBLIOGRAPHY

Acker, Joan. 1988. "Class, Gender, and the Relations of Distribution." *Signs* 13 (3): 473-497.

Aldrich, Howard. 1989. "Networking Among Women Entrepreneurs." Pp. 102-132 in Oliver Hagen, Carol Rivchun, and Donald Sexton, eds. *Women-Owned Businesses.* New York: Praeger.

Aldrich, Howard, Amanda Elam Brickman and Patricia Reese. 1995. "Strong Ties, Weak Ties, and Strangers: Do Women Differ From Men in Their Use of Networking to Obtain Assistance?" Paper, Department of Sociology, University of North Carolina at Chapel Hill.

Aldrich, Howard, and Nina Liou. 1995. "The Invisible {woman} Entrepreneur: Lack of Attention to Women Owners in the Academic,Business and Popular Press." Paper, Department of Sociology and Kenan-Flagler School of Business, University of North Carolina, Chapel Hill.

Aldrich, Howard, and Jeffrey Pfeffer. 1976. "Environments of Organizations." Pp. 79-105 *Annual Review of Sociology.* (2): 79-105.

Aldrich, Howard, Pat Ray Reese and Paola Dubini. 1989. "Women On the Verge of a Breakthrough: Networking Among Entrepreneurs in the United States and Italy." *Entrepreneurship and Regional Development* (1): 339-356.

Aldrich, Howard, and B. Rosen and W. Woodward. 1986. "Social Behavior and Entrepreneurial Networks," in *Frontiers of Entrepreneurship Research* (1): 239-240.

Aldrich, Howard, and Roger Waldinger. 1990. "Ethnicity and Entrepreneurship." In *Annual Review of Sociology* (16): 111-135.

Aldrich, Howard, Catherine Zimmer, and Trevor Jones. 1986. "Small Business Still Speaks With the Same Voice: A Replication of the 'Voice of Small Business and the Politics of Survival'." *Sociological Review* 34 (May): 335-356.

Amsden, Alice H. (ed.). 1980. *The Economics of Women and Work.* New York: St. Martins Press.

Anderson, Benedict. 1991. *Imagined Communities: Reflections on the Origins and Spread of Nationalism.* New York: Verso.

Appelbaum, Eileen. 1987. "Restructuring Work: Temporary, Part-Time, and At-Home Employment." Pp. 268-309 in National Research Council and Heidi Hartmann (ed.) *Computer Chips and Paper Clips: Technology and Women's Employment.* Washington, D.C.: National Academy Press.

Aronson, Robert L. 1991. *Self-Employment: A Labor Market Perspective.* Ithaca, NY: Cornell University Press.

The Bank of New York (NJ). 1995. "2nd Annual Report on the State of Small Business in New Jersey." Market Research Institute, October.

Barnett, H.G. 1953. *Innovation: The Basis of Cultural Change.* New York: McGraw-Hill.

Bates, Timothy. 1990. "Entrepreneur Human Capital Inputs and Small Business Longevity." *The Review of Economics and Statistics* 72 (November) 4: 551-559.

Bechhofer, Frank and Brian Elliott, eds. 1981. *The Petite Bourgeoisie: Comparative Studies of the Uneasy Stratum*. New York: St. Martin's Press.

Beechey, Veronia. 1987. *Unequal Work*. London: Verso.

Beneria, Lourdes and Catherine R. Stimpson, eds. 1987. *Women, Households, and the Economy*. New Brunswick: Rutgers University Press.

Berger, Bridget, ed. 1991. *The Culture of Entrepreneurship*. San Francisco: ICS Press.

Biggart, Nicole Woolsey. 1989. *Charismatic Capitalism: Direct Selling Organizations in America*. Chicago: The University of Chicago Press.

Birch, David L. 1987. *Job Creation in America: How Our Smallest Companies Put the Most People to Work*. New York: The Free Press.

Blackford, Mansel G. 1991. *A History of Small Business In America*. New York: Twaynes Publishers.

Blau, David M. 1987. "A Time-Series Analysis of Self-Employment in the United States." *Journal of Political Economy* 95 (3): 445-467.

Bluestone, Barry, and Bennett Harrison. 1982. *The Deindustrialization of America*. New York: Basic Books.

Bluestone, Barry, and Bennett Harrison. 1990. "Wage Polarisation in the US and the Flexibility Debate." *Cambridge Journal of Economics* 14 (1990): 351-373.

Bluestone, Barry, and Sarah Kuhn. 1987. "Economic Restructuring and the Female Labor Market: The Impact of Industrial Change On Women." Pp. 3-32 in L. Beneria and C. Stimpson eds. *Women, Households and the Economy*. New Brunswick: Rutgers University Press.

Boden, Richard Joseph, Jr. 1990. *Gender Differences in Entrepreneurial Selection and Performance*. Ph.D. Dissertation, University of Maryland College Park.

Bonacich, Edna. 1972. "A Theory of Middleman Minorities." *American Sociological Review* 38 (October): 583-594.

Bonacich, Edna, and Ivan Light. 1988. *Immigrant Entrepreneurs: Koreans in Los Angeles, 1965-1982*. Berkeley: University of California Press.

Bonacich, Edna, and John Modell. 1980. *The Economic Basis of Ethnic Solidarity: Small Business In the Japanese American Community*. Berkeley: University of California Press.

Braudel, Fernand. 1982. *The Wheels of Commerce, Civilization and Capitalism 15th-18th Century, vols. 1-3*. Translation by Sian Reynolds. New York: Harper and Row.

Brophy, David J. 1989. "Financing Women-Owned Entrepreneurial Firms." Pp. 55-75 in Oliver Hagen, Carol Rivchun, and Donald Sexton, eds. *Women -Owned Businesses*. New York: Praeger.

Brown, Linda Keller. 1981. *The Woman Manager in the United States: A Research Analysis and Bibliography*. Washington, D.C.: Business and Professional Women's Foundation.

Bruchey, Stuart W. 1980. *Small Business in American Life*. New York: Columbia University Press.

Brusco, Sebastiano. 1982. "The Emilian Model: Productive Decentralisation and Social Integration." *Cambridge Journal of Economics*. (6): 167-184.

Butler, John Sibley. 1991. *Entrepreneurship and Self-Help Among Black Americans.* Albany, NY: State University of New York Press.

Butler, John Sibley and Patricia Greene. 1996. "The Minority Community as Small Business Incubator." *Journal of Small Business Research* (Spring). Author's Draft.

Bygrave, William D. (ed.). 1994. *The Portable MBA in Entrepreneurship.* New York: John Wiley & Sons.

Chandler, Alfred. 1994. *Scale and Scope: The Dynamics of Industrial Capitalism.* Cambridge, MA: Harvard University Press.

Charlboneau, Jill F. 1981. "The Woman Entrepreneur." *American Demographics* (June): 21-23.

Cochran, Thomas C. 1968. "Entrepreneurship." Pp. 87-91 in David Sills (ed.) *The International Encyclopedia of Social Sciences.* New York: Macmillan and The Free Press.

Cockburn, Cynthia. 1985. *Machinery of Dominance: Women, Men and Technical Know-How.* London: Pluto Press.

Collins, Orvis, and David Moore. 1970. *The Organization Makers: A Behavioral Study of Independent Entrepreneurs.* New York: Meredith.

Coontz, Stephanie and Peta Henderson. 1986. *Women's Work, Men's Property: The Origins of Gender and Class* . London: Verso.

Coser, Rose Laub. 1991. *In Defense of Modernity: Role Complexity and Individual Autonomy.* Stanford: Stanford University Press.

Cooley, Charles Horton. [1902] 1998. *On Self and Social Organization.* Chicago: University of Chicago Press.

Cott, Nancy. 1978. *The Bonds of True Womanhood: Woman's Sphere in New England, 1780-1835.* New Haven, CT: Yale University Press.

Cromie, Stanley. 1987. "Motivations of Aspiring Male and Female Entrepreneurs." *Journal of Occupational Behaviour* (8): 251-261.

Crompton, Rosemary, and Michael Mann, eds. 1986. *Gender and Stratification.* Cambridge: Polity Press.

Crosby, Faye J. (ed.). 1987. *Spouse, Parent, Worker: On Gender and Multiple Roles.* New Haven: Yale University Press.

———. 1993. *Juggling: The Unexpected Advantages of Balancing Career and Home for Women and Their Families.* New York: The Free Press.

Dean, James W. 1987. *Deciding to Innovate: How Firms Justify Advanced Technology.* Cambridge, MA: Ballinger.

Deaux, Kay. 1987. "Psychological Constructions of Masculinity and Femininity." Pp. 289-303. In June M. Reinisch, L. Rosenblum and S. Sanders (eds.) *Masculinity/Femininity: Basic Perspectives.* New York: Oxford University Press.

Deaux, Kay and Mary E. Kite. 1987. "Thinking About Gender." Beth B. Hess and M. M. Ferree (eds.) *Analyzing Gender: A Handbook of Social Science Research.* Beverly Hills, CA: Sage.

Deaux, Kay and Marianne Lafrance. 1998. "Chapter Seventeen: Gender." Gilbert, Daniel T., Susan T. Fiske, and Gardner Lindzey (Eds.) *The Handbook of Social Psychology.* Volume One. New York: Oxford University Press and The McGraw Hill Company.

Deaux, Kay, and Brenda Major. 1990. "A Social Psychology Model of Gender." Pp. 89-113 in D. Rhode (Ed.) *Theoretical Perspectives on Sexual Difference*. New Haven, CT: Yale University Press.

DeSoto, Hernando. 1989. *The Other Path: The Invisible Revolution in the Third World*. Translation by June Abbott. New York: Harper & Row.

Dolinsky, Arthur L., Richard K. Caputo and Kishore Pasumarty. 1993. "The Effects of Education on Business Ownership: A Longitudinal Study of Women," *Entrepreneurship Theory and Practice* 18 (1) (Fall): 43-53.

Dolinsky, Arthur L., Richard K. Caputo and Kishore Pasumarty. 1994. "Long-term Entrepreneurial Patterns: A National Study of Black and White Female Entry and Stayer Status Differences." (January): 18-26.

Drucker, Peter F. 1985. *Innovation and Entrepreneurship: Practises and Principles*. New York: Harper & Row.

Dubini, Paola and Howard Aldrich. 1991. "Personal and Extended Networks Are Essential to the Entrepreneurial Process." *Journal of Business Venturing*. 6 (5) (September): 305-313.

Dunn, Thomas Albert and Douglas Holtz-Eakin. 1995. "Capital Market Constraints, Parental Wealth and the Transition to Self-Employment Among Men and Women." National Longitudinal Survey Discussion Paper No 96-29. Distributed by the U.S. Department of Labor Statistics.

Eagly, Alice H. 1987. *Sex Differences in Social Behavior: A Social Role Interpretation*. Hillsdale, NJ: Lawrence Erlbaum Associates.

Eagly, Alice H., and Shelly Chaiken. 1993. *The Psychology of Attitudes*. New York: Harcourt Brace Jovanovich.

Eagly, Alice H., and Blair T. Johnson. 1990. "Gender and Leadership Style: A Meta-Analysis." *Psychological Bulletin* 108 (2): 233-256.

Engels, Frederick. 1884 [1942]. *The Origin of the Family, Private Property and the State*. New York: International Publishers.

England, Paula and George Farcas. 1986. *Households, Enmployment and Gender: A Social, Economic and Demographic View*. Chicago: Aldine de Gruyter.

Enkelis, Liane, and Karen Olson. 1995. *On Our Own Terms: Portraits of Women Business Owners*. San Francisco: Berret-Koehler.

Epstein, Cynthia Fuchs. 1970. *Woman's Place: Options and Limits in Professional Careers*. Berkeley: University of California Press.

———. 1974. "Ambiguity as Social Control: Women In Professional Elites." Pp. 26-38 in Phyllis Steward and Muriel G. Cantor (eds.) *Varieties of Work Experience*. New York: Schenkman.

———. 1981. *Women In Law*. New York: Basic Books.

———. 1988. *Deceptive Distinctions: Sex, Gender and the Social Order*. New Haven: Yale University Press.

———. 1988. "Multiple Demands and Multiple Roles: The Conditions of Successful Management." Pp. 23-35 in F.J. Crosby, Ed. *Spouse, Parent, Worker: On Gender and Multiple Roles*. New Haven: Yale University Press.

———. 1989. "Workplace Boundaries: Conceptions and Creations." *Social Research* 56 (Autumn): 571-590.

———. 1992. "Tinkerbells and Pinups: The Construction and Reconstruction of Gender Boundaries at Work." Pp. 232-256 in Michele Lamont and Marcel Fournier, eds. *Cultivating Differences: Symbolic Boudaries and the Making of Inequality.* Chicago: University of Chicago Press.

Epstein, Cynthia Fuchs, and Rose Laub Coser (eds.). 1981. *Access to Power: Cross-National Studies of Women and Elites.* London: George Allen & Unwin.

Epstein, Cynthia Fuchs and Kimberly A. Reed. 1997. "Changes in Structure, Changes in the Self." Pp. 128-152 in Kaisa Kauppinen-Toropainen and Tuula Gordon, eds. *Unresolved Dilemmas: Women, Work and Family in the United States, Europe and the Soviet Union.* Great Britain: Avebury.

Evans, David S. and Linda S. Leighton. 1989. "Some Empirical Aspects of Entrepreneurship." *The American Economic Review* 79 (June)3: 519-535.

Farkas, George, and Paula England, eds. 1988. *Industries, Firms and Jobs: Sociological and Economic Approaches.* New York: Plenum Press.

Ferber, Marianne A. and Julie A. Nelson, eds. 1993. *Beyond Economic Man: Feminist Theory and Economics.* Chicago: University of Chicago Press.

Fiol, C. Marlene, and Howard Aldrich. 1993. "Collusion or Collision? Exploring the Boundaries of Family Business." Conference on Family Business, University of California at Los Angeles, March 18-20.

Franke, George R., Deborah F. Crown, and Deborah F. Spake. 1997. "Gender Differences in Ethical Perceptions of Business Practices: A Social Role Theory Perspective." *Journal of Applied Psychology.* 82 (6): 920-934.

Freeman, Elizabeth Byrne, and J. Kay Keels. 1992. "A Framework of Entrepreneurial Networking." American Academy of Management, Meetings, August 1992.

Fried, Frank, Harris, Shriver and Jacobson. 1995. "Fair Lending Time Line." [Online]. Available: http//www.ffhsj.com/fairlend/timetest.htm [1998, January 26].

Gabor, Andrea. 1995. "Crashing the 'Old Boy' Party: Boston's A Team is Far More Than a Network of Career Women." *New York Times* Section 3, Sunday, January 8, 1995, pp. 1, 6.

Gerson, Kathleen. 1985. *Hard Choices: How Women Decide About Work, Career, and Motherhood.* Berkeley: University of California Press.

Gilbert, Neil. 1995. *Welfare Justice: Restoring Social Equity.* New Haven: Yale University Press.

Ginsburg, Faye. 1989. *Contested Lives.* Berkeley: University of California Press.

Ginsberg, Faye and Anna Lowenhaupt Tsing. 1990. *Uncertain Terms: Negotiating Gender in American Culture.* Boston: Beacon Press.

Glassford, Margaret. 1991. "The State and Liberal Feminism: The Ontario Government's Business Ownership Program For Women." Paper, American Sociological Association, Cinncinati, OH.

Godfrey, Joline. 1992. *Our Wildest Dreams: Women Entrepreneurs Making Money, Having Fun, Doing Good.* New York: Harper Collins.

Goffee, Robert and Richard Scase. 1985. *Women in Charge: The Experiences of Female Entrepreneurs.* Boston: Allen & Unwin.

Goffman, Erving. 1959. *The Presentation of Self in Everyday Life.* New York: DoubleDay/ Anchor Books.

————. 1967. *Interaction Ritual.* New York: Anchor Books.

Gordon, David M., Richard Edwards, and Michael Reich. 1982. *Segmented Work, Divided Workers.* Cambridge University Press.

Granovetter, Mark. 1974, 1995. *Getting a Job: A Study of Contacts and Careers.* 2nd Edition. Chicago: University of Chicago Press.

Granovetter, Mark. 1984. "Small Is Bountiful: Labor Markets and Establishment Size." *American Sociological Review* 49 (June): 323-334.

Granovetter, Mark. 1985. "Economic Action and Social Structure: The Problem of Embeddedness." *American Journal of Sociology* 91: 481-510.

Greene, Patricia and Margaret A. Johnson. 1995. "Social Learning and Middleman Minority Theory: Explanations for Self-Employed Women." *National Journal of Sociology* 9, 1 (Summer): 59-84.

Greene, Patricia. 1995. "Women Entrepreneurs: A Consideration of Capital Types." Conference on Immigrant and Minority Entrepreneurship, Austin, TX.

Gregory, Charles. "Horatio Alger, Jr. 1832-99." Pp. 7-8 in Justin Wintle, ed. *Makers of Nineteenth Century Culture: 1800-1914.* Boston: Routledge & Kegan Paul.

Hagen, Oliver, Carol Rivchun, and Donald Sexton, eds. 1989. *Women Owned Businesses.* New York: Praeger.

Hartmann, Heidi. 1976. "Capitalism, Patriarchy and Job Segregation by Sex." Pp. 137-169 in M. Blaxall and B. Reagan (eds.) *Women and the Workplace.* Chicago: University of Chicago Press.

Hartsock, Nancy C. M. 1983. *Money, Sex and Power: Toward A Feminist Historical Materialism.* New York: New York University Press.

Helgesen, Sally. 1989. *The Female Advantage—Women's Ways of Leadership.* New York: 1990.

Hisrich Robert D. 1989. "Women Entrepreneurs: Problems and Prescriptions for Success in the Future." Pp. 3-32 in Oliver Hagen, Carol Rivchun, and Donald Sexton, eds. *Women-Owned Businesses.* New York: Praeger.

Hisrich, Robert D. and Candida Brush. 1986. *The Woman Entrepreneur: Starting, Managing, and Financing a Successful New Business.* Lexington, MA: Lexington Books, D.C. Heath.

Hochschild, Arlie with Brenda Machung. 1989. *The Second Shift.* New York: Viking.

Hodson, Randy and Teresa Sullivan. 1995. *The Social Organization of Work.* 2nd Edition. CA: Wadsworth Publishing Company.

Horrell, Sara, and Jill Rubery. 1991. "Gender and Working Time: An Analysis of Employers' Working-Time Policies." *Cambridge Journal of Economics* 15 (1991): 373-391.

Howell, Martha C. 1986. *Women, Production and Patriarchy in Late Medieval Cities.* Chicago: University of Chicago Press.

Hughes, Jonathan. 1986. *The Vital Few: The Entrepreneur & American Economic Progress.* New York: Oxford University Press.

Jackall, Robert. 1989. *Moral Mazes: The Lives of Corporate Managers.* New York: Oxford University Press.

Jacobs, Jerry A. 1989. *Revolving Doors: Sex Segregation in Women's Careers.* Palo

Alto, CA: Standford University Press.

Judd, Richard J., William T. Greenwood, and Fred Becker, eds. 1988. *Small Business in a Regulated Economy: Issues and Policy Implications.* New York: Quorum Books.

Kanter, Rosabeth Moss. 1977. *Men and Women of the Corporation.* New York: Basic Books.

Kaplan, Gilbert E. (ed.). 1988. *The Way It Was: An Oral History of Finance 1967-1987.* New York: William Morrow.

Kent, Calvin, Donald Sexton, and Karl Vesper, eds. 1982. *Encyclopedia of Entrepreneurship.* Englewood Cliffs, NJ: Prentice Hall.

Kirzner, Israel M. 1979. *Perception, Opportunity, and Profit: Studies in the Theory of Entrepreneurship.* Chicago: University of Chicago.

Kogan, Nathan and Karen Dorros. 1978. "Sex Differences in Risk-Taking and Its Attribution." *Sex Roles* 4 (5): 763.

Kohn, Melvin I., and Carmi Schooler, eds. 1983. *Work and Personality: An Inquiry Into the Impact of Social Stratification.* Norwood, NJ: Ablex Publishing Co.

Kohn, Melvin I., and Kazmierz M. Slomczynski. 1990. *Social Structure and Self-Direction: A Comparative Analysis of the United States and Poland.* Cambridge, MA: Harvard University Press.

Korn/Ferry International. 1993. "Decade of the Executive Woman." University of California Los Angeles. Graduate School of Management.

Krecker, Margaret L., and Angela M. O'Rand. 1991. "Contested Milieux: Small Firms, Unionization, and the Provision of Protective Structures." *Sociological Forum* (6): 93-117.

Light, Ivan. 1972. *Ethnic Enterprise in America.* Berkeley: University of California Press.

Lindesmith, Alfred, Anselm L. Strauss, Norman K. Denzin. 1988. *Social Psychology.* Sixth ed. Englewood Cliffs, NJ: Prentice Hall.

Lipset, Seymour Martin, Martin Trow and James Coleman. 1956. *Union Democracy.* New York: The Free Press/Anchor Books.

Lo, Clarence Y. H. 1990. *Small Property Versus Big Government: Social Origins of the Property Tax Revolt.* Los Angeles, CA: University of California Press.

Lorber, Judith. 1994. *Paradoxes of Gender.* New Haven: Yale University Press.

———. 1984. *Women Phycisians: Careers, Status and Power.* New York: Tavistock.

Loscocco, Karyn A. 1996. "Gender and the Work-Family Nexus Among the Self-Employed." Paper. Eastern Sociological Association Annual Meeting.

Loscocco, Karyn A. and Keven T. Leicht. 1993. "Gender, Work-Family Linkages, and Economic Success Among Small Business Owners." *Journal of Marriage and the Family* 55 (November): 875-887.

Loscocco, Karyn A., and Joyce Robinson. 1991. "Barriers to Women's Small-Business Success in the United States." *Gender and Society* 5 (4) (December): 511-532.

Loscocco, Karyn A., Joyce Robinson, Richard K. Hall, and John K. Allen. 1991. "Gender and Small Business Success: An Inquiry into Women's Relative Disadvantage," *Social Forces* 70 (1)(September): 65-85.

Marx, Karl. 1887, 1965. *Capital: A Critical Analysis of Capitalist Production.* Vol. 1. Frederick Engels, ed. New York: International Publishers.

McClelland, David C. 1962. "Business Drive and National Achievement," *Harvard Business Review* 40 (July-Aug): 104-106.

———. 1961. *The Achieving Society.* Princeton, NJ: D. Van Nostrand Co.

Medoff, James, Charles Brown, and James Hamilton. 1990. *Employers Large and Small.* Cambridge: Harvard University Press.

Merton, Robert K. [1949, 1957, 1968]. *Social Theory and Social Structure.* Glencoe, IL:Free Press.

———. 1968. "The Matthew Effect in Sciences." *Science* (159): 56-63.

Merton, Robert K., Marjorie Fiske, and Patricia Kendall. 1990. *The Focused Interview: A Manual of Problems and Procedures.* Second Edition. New York: The Free Press.

Merton, Robert K., Alice S. Kitt. 1950. "Contributions to the Theory of Reference Group Behavior." in Robert K. Merton and Paul Lazarsfeld (eds.) *Continuities in Social Research: Studies in the Scope and Method of the American Soldier.* Glencoe, IL: The Free Press.

Mills, C. W. 1953. *White Collar.* New York: Oxford University Press.

National Foundation For Women Business Owners. 1992. *Women Owned Businesses: The New Economic Force.* Data Report. Washington, D.C.: National Foundation For Women Business Owners.

———. 1994. *Compendium of Statistics on Women-Owned Businesses in the U.S.* Washington, D.C.: National Foundation For Women Business Owners.

———. 1994. *Credibility, Creativity, and Independence: The Greatest Challenges and Biggest Rewards of Business Ownership Among Women.* Report Sponsored by AT&T and MetLife.

———. 1994. New Study Quantifies Thinking and Management Differences Between Women and Men Business Owners. PressRelease. Http://www.nfwbo.org/rr003.htm [1997, July 8].

———. 1995. "2020 Vision: Entrepreneurial Policies for the 21st Century." Report. (July 11): 2

New Jersey State Legislature, Assembly Economic Growth, Agriculture, Tourism and Coastal Protection Committee, and Assembly Commerce and Regulated Professions Committee. 1991. *A Small Business Summit to Evaluate Conditions Surrounding Small Business in New Jersey.* (March 20, 1991) Public Information Office, Trenton, NJ.

Newman, Katherine S. 1993. *Declining Fortunes: The Withering of the American Dream.* New York: Basic Books.

Park, Kyeyoung. 1997. *The Korean American Dream: Immigrants and Small Business in New York City.* New York: Cornell University Press.

Parkin, Frank. 1974. "Strategies of Social Closure in Class Formation," in Parkin, ed. *The Social Analysis of Class Structure.* The British Sociological Association. London: Tavistock Publications.

Parsons, Talcott. 1951. *The Social System.* New York: The Free Press.

Perrow, Charles. 1990. "Small Firm Networks." New York: Russell Sage Foundation.

Peterson, Richard L. 1981. "An Investigation of Sex Discrimination in Commercial Bank Lending." *Bell Journal of Economics* 12 (Autumn): 547-561.

Phizacklea, Annie. 1988. "Entrepreneurship, Ethnicity, and Gender," Pp. 20-33 in Sally Westwood and P. Bhachu, eds. *Enterprising Women*. New York: Routledge.

Piore, Michael J. 1988. "The Changing Role of Small Business in the U.S. Economy." Paper for the Project on "New Industrial Organization" of the Institute of Labour Studies of the International Labour Organization.

Piore, Michael J. and Charles Sable. 1984. *The Second Industrial Divide: Possibilities For Prosperity*. New York: Basic Books.

Polodny, Joel. 1991. "The Matthew Effect and the Constraints of Status: A Sociological Perspective On Markets." American Sociological Association Annual Meeting, Cinncinati, Ohio.

Pringle, Rosemary. 1989. *Secretaries Talk: Sexuality, Power and Work*. New York: Verso.

Reskin, Barbara and Heidi Hartmann (Eds.) 1986. *Women's Work, Men's Work: Sex Segreagation on the Job*. Washington, D.C.: National Academy Press.

Reskin, Barbara and Patricia Roos. 1990. *Job Queues, Gender Queues: Explaining Inroads Into Male Occupations*. Philadelphia: Temple University Press.

Ridgeway, Cecilia L. (Ed.) 1992. *Gender, Interaction and Inequality*. New York: Springer-Verlag.

Romanelli, Elaine. 1991. "The Evolution of New Organizational Forms." *Annual Review of Sociology* (17): 79-103.

Rosener, Judith. 1990. "Ways Women Lead." *Harvard Business Review*. 68 (November-December): 119-125.

Salais, Robert, and Michael Storper. 1992. "The Four Worlds of Contemporary Industry." *Cambridge Journal of Economics* (16): 169-193.

Schumpeter, Joseph A. 1942. *Capitalism, Socialism and Democracy*. New York: Harper and Rowe.

———. 1974. *The Theory of Economic Development*. New York: Oxford University Press.

———. 1989. *Essays on Entrepreneurs, Innovations, Business Cycles, and the Evolution of Capitalism*. Richard V. Clemence (ed.). New Brunswick, NJ: Transaction.

Schwartz, Eleanor. 1986. "Entrepreneurship: A New Female Frontier." *Journal of Contemporary Business* (Winter): 47-76.

Scollard, Jeannette R. 1985. *The Self-Employed Woman*. New York: Simon and Schuster.

Scott, Allen J. and Michael Storper, eds. 1988. *Production, Work, Territory: The Geographical Anatomy of Industrial Capitalism*. London: Unwin Hyman.

Scott, James C. 1990. *Domination and the Arts of Resistance: Hidden Transcripts*. New Haven: Yale University Press.

Searle, G. R. 1993. *Entrepreneurial Politics in Mid-Victorian Britain*. New York: Oxford University Press.

Sexton, Donald L. 1989. "Growth Decisions and Growth Patterns of Women-Owned Enterprises," Pp. 135-150 in Oliver Hagen, Carol Rivchun, and

Donald Sexton, eds. *Women-Owned Businesses*. New York: Praeger.

————. 1989. "Research On Women-Owned Businesses: Current Status and Future Directions," Pp. 183-193 in Oliver Hagen, Carol Rivchun, and Donald Sexton (eds.) *Women-Owned Businesses*. New York: Praeger.

Shapero, Albert and Lisa Sokol. 1982. "Social Dimensions of Entrepreneurship." Pp. 72-90. In Kent, Sexton and Vespers, eds. *Encyclopedia of Entrepreneurship*. Englewood Cliffs, NJ: Prentice Hall.

Sills, David. 1968. "Voluntary Association." In David L. Sills, ed. *International Encyclopedia of the Social Sciences*. (16): 357-379.

Skolnick, Arlene. 1993. *Embattled Paradise: The American Family in an Age of Uncertainty*. New York: Basic Books.

Smeltzer, L.R. and G.L. Fann. 1989. "Gender Differences in External Networks of Small Owner Managers." *Journal of Small Business Management* (27): 25-32.

Stacey, Judith. 1990. *Brave New Families*. New York: Basic Books.

Steinmetz, George, and Erik Olin Wright. 1989. "The Fall and Rise of the Petty Bourgeoisie: Changing Patterns of Self-Employment in the Postwar United States." *American Journal of Sociology* 94 (5)(March): 973-1018.

Stets, Jan E. And Peter J. Burke. 1996. "Gender, Control and Interaction. "*Social Psychology Quarterly* 59 (3): 193-220.

Storper, Michael. 1989. "The Transition to Flexible Specialisation in the US Film Industry: External Economies, the Division of Labour, and the Crossing of Industrial Divides." *Cambridge Journal of Economics* (13): 273-305.

Swidler, Ann. 1986. "Culture in Action: Symbols and Strategies." *American Sociological Review* 51 (April): 273-286.

Szelenyi, Ivan. 1988. *Socialist Entrepreneurs: Embourgeoisement in Rural Hungary*. Madison: University of Wisconsin Press.

Tausig, Micheal and J. Michello. 1988. "Seeking Social Support." *Basic and Applied Social Psychology*. 9 (1): 1-12.

Tilly, Lousie A. And Charles Tilly, eds. 1981. *Class Conflict and Collective Action*. Beverly Hills, CA: Sage Publications.

Tilly, Louise A. and Joan W. Scott. 1978. *Women, Work, & Family*. New York: Holt, Rinehart, and Winston.

Tocqueville, Alexis de. 1990. *Democracy in America, Volume One*. [1835, 1945] New York: Vintage Books.

United States Department of Commerce. 1978a. *The Bottom Line: Equal Enterprise in America: Report of the President's Interagency Task Force on Women Business Owners*. Washington,D.C.: U.S. Government Printing Office.

United States Department of Commerce. 1992, 1987, 1982, 1977, 1972. *Census of Women-Owned Businesses*. Washington, D.C.: U.S. Government Printing Office.

United States Department of Commerce. 1987. *Characteristics of Business Owners*. Washington, D.C.: U.S. Government Printing Office.

United States Department of Commerce. 1986. *Women and Business Ownership: An Annotated Bibliography*. Washington, D.C.: U.S. Government Printing Office.

United States Department of The Treasury. 1978. *Credit and Capital Formation: a Report to the President's Interagency Task Force on Women Business Owners.* U.S. Small Business Administration, Washington, D.C.: U.S. Government Printing Office.

United States Small Business Administration. 1991, 1990, 1989, 1985, 1982. *The State of Small Business: A Report to the President.* Washington, D.C.: U.S. Government Printing Office.

United States Small Business Administration. Office of Advocacy. "Facts About Small Business." [1996] http://www.sba.gov/ADVO/stats/fact1.html [January 26, 1998].

United States Small Business Administration. Office of Advocacy. Small Business Answer Card. [1997] http://www.sba.gov/ADVO/stats/answer.html [January 26, 1998].

Vogel, David. 1989. *Fluctuating Fortunes: The Politcal Power of Business in America.* New York: Basic Books.

Weber, Max. 1911. "Geschaftsbericht." *Deutscher Sociologentag Verhandlungen* (1): 39-62. Quoted in David Sills. "Voluntary Association." in *The International Encyclopedia of Social Science.* (16): 362-379.

———. 1930. *The Protestant Ethic and the Spirit of Capitalism.* Translated by Talcott Parsons. Introduction to 1985 edition by Anthony Giddens. London: Allen & Unwin.

———. 1978. *Economy and Society Volumes 1 & 2.* Guenther Roth and Claus Wittich (eds.). Berkeley: University of California Press.

Weiss, Linda. 1988. *Creating Capitalism: The State and Small Business Since 1945.* New York: Basil Blackwell.

West, Candace and Don H. Zimmerman. 1987. "Doing Gender." *Gender and Society* (1): 125-151.

Weiwel, W. And A. Hunter. 1985. "The Interorganizational Network as a Resource." *Administrative Science Quarterly* (30): 482-496.

Westwood, Sallie. 1985. *All Day Every Day: Factory and Family in the Making of Women's Lives.* Urbana, IL: University of Illinois Press.

Westwood, Sallie, and Parminder Bhachu. 1988. *Enterprising Women: Ethnicity, Economy, and Gender Relations.* New York: Routledge.

Wilkens, Joanne. 1987. *Her Own Business: Success Secrets of Entrepreneurial Women.* New York: McGraw-Hill.

Wright, Erik Olin. 1985. *Classes.* London: Verso.

Zelizer, Viviana A. 1994. *The Social Meaning of Money.* New York: Basic Books.

Zukin, Sharon, and Paul DiMaggio, eds. 1990. *Structures of Capital: The Social Organization of the Economy.* New York: Cambridge University Press.

Index